AF687696

Options and Derivatives Mastery

Crafting Strategies for Market Dominance

Nathan Venture, D

Copyright 2026 All rights reserved.

No part of this book may be reproduced in any form or by any electronic or mechanical means including information storage and retrieval systems, without permission in writing from the author. The only exception is by a reviewer, who may quote short excerpts in a review.

Although the author and publisher have made every effort to ensure that the information in this book was correct at press time, the author and publisher do not assume and hereby disclaim any liability to any party for any loss, damage, or disruption caused by errors or omissions, whether such errors or omissions result from negligence, accident, or any other cause.

This publication is designed to provide accurate and authoritative information with regard to the subject matter covered. It is sold with the understanding that the publisher is not engaged in rendering professional services. If legal advice or other expert assistance is required, the services of a competent professional should be sought.

The fact that an organization or website is referred to in this work as a citation and/or a potential source of further information does not mean that the author or the publisher endorses the information the organization or website may provide or recommendations it may make.

Please remember that Internet websites listed in this work may have changed or disappeared between when this work was written and when it is read.

Contents

Introduction

Before any strategy can be evaluated on expected return, it has to be judged on whether it can survive the market in which it will actually be traded. Derivatives are not abstract pricing objects; they are contracts embedded in a market structure that can widen, fragment, or seize up precisely when their leverage becomes most consequential. The same instrument that appears highly efficient in calm conditions may become difficult to hedge, expensive to roll, or impossible to exit when liquidity thins and correlations move toward one. That is why liquidity is not a secondary concern but a primary design constraint.

In practice, liquidity has several dimensions. A contract may trade with heavy displayed volume yet still be costly to use if the spread is wide, depth disappears after the top of book, or size moves the market. A market may quote continuously while still being fragile if participants are concentrated, financing is short term, or positions are crowded in the same direction. During stress, the issue is rarely just price discovery; it is the interaction between funding, margin, and the ability to transfer risk. Episodes of market turmoil have shown how quickly uncertainty about where risk resides can intensify into broader instability [1][4][10].

For the derivatives practitioner, this means that the best structure on paper is not necessarily the best structure in execution. A clean hedge with attractive convexity can become inferior to a less elegant alternative if it requires frequent rebalancing in an illiquid contract. A spread that looks limited-risk can still create meaningful liquidity risk if one leg is easy to transact and the other is not. Even in exchange-traded products, the apparent simplicity of standardized contracts can mask differences in market depth across expirations, strikes, and underlyings. In OTC markets, the challenge expands further because liquidity is often relationship-based, quote-driven, and dependent on dealer balance sheet capacity.

Market structure also shapes how information is incorporated into prices. Exchanges centralize order flow, standardize terms, and provide transparent quoting, clearing, and margining. That architecture tends to reduce bilateral credit exposure and improve comparability across participants. OTC markets, by contrast, offer customization. They can match notional size, maturity, payoff profile, or embedded optionality to a specific need that listed contracts cannot replicate. The trade-off is that customization often comes with less transparency, more negotiation, and greater dependence on counterparties, documentation, and collateral discipline.

This distinction matters because derivatives are used not only to express views, but to transfer exposures that are already embedded in a business, a portfolio, or a liability structure. A commodity producer may need a hedge that aligns with physical delivery timing and quality differentials. A pension plan may need duration exposure that fits a liability profile rather than a benchmark. A macro fund may need a rate structure that matches a view on the shape of the curve. In each case, the choice between exchange-traded and OTC instruments is not merely operational; it determines how precisely the exposure can be shaped and how much residual basis risk remains.

Liquidity is closely linked to the behavior of leverage. Derivatives allow a small amount of capital to control a much larger underlying exposure, which is useful precisely because it is efficient. But leverage also compresses the margin for error. When markets move against a position, the need to post collateral or reduce exposure can force trading at unfavorable prices. This creates a feedback loop: losses trigger margin calls, margin calls trigger sales, sales pressure prices, and falling prices can trigger more calls. The result is not just mark-to-market volatility but a financing problem that can alter the path of the market itself [1][6][10].

For this reason, the operational realities of clearing and collateral management are inseparable from strategy selection. A position that is theoretically hedged may still generate large cash demands if its components settle differently, reprice at different speeds, or consume margin asymmetrically. A portfolio that is net neutral in directional terms may still be exposed to liquidity stress if the instruments used to achieve that neutrality require frequent adjustment. Risk managers therefore have to think beyond delta and volatility and consider the funding profile of the hedge, the concentration of counterparties, and the behavior of margin requirements under stress.

Convexity adds another layer. One of the main attractions of derivatives is that they can create nonlinearity: limited downside with substantial upside, or a payoff that accelerates when the market moves through a threshold. That nonlinearity is valuable because it allows investors to define risk in advance or to target specific market states. Yet convexity is not free. It is typically purchased through premium, financing, or the acceptance of adverse path dependence. The market rarely gives away favorable asymmetry without charging for it somewhere else, whether through time decay, implied volatility, bid-ask spread, or rebalancing cost.

The practical implication is that flexibility must be treated as a resource with a price. The ability to tailor exposure is one of the defining strengths of derivatives, but customization increases complexity. The more precisely a structure is matched to a view or a risk, the more carefully it must be monitored for secondary effects: skew exposure, term structure exposure, correlation exposure, and liquidity dependence. A position can be directionally correct and still disappoint because the wrong part of the volatility surface moved, or because the hedge was built on an assumption of continuous liquidity that did not hold.

That is why sophisticated derivative use requires a shift in perspective. The question is not simply, "What is the payoff?" but also, "How does the payoff behave under stress, and what market conditions are needed for it to function as intended?" In calm markets, many structures appear interchangeable. Under pressure, the differences become visible: the contract that rolls cleanly, the hedge that preserves funding flexibility, the structure that can be unwound without moving the market, and the position that fails because its liquidity assumptions were implicit rather than tested.

In the sections that follow, the focus will move from this market architecture to the instruments themselves. But the point remains constant: derivatives are tools whose value depends as much on market structure, financing, and execution as on theoretical payoff. Any serious use of them begins with that recognition.

CHAPTER 1

Chapter 1: The Derivatives Landscape and the Investor's Edge

Before the mechanics of each contract are separated and compared, it helps to frame derivatives as the market's language for transferring exposure, not merely adding complexity. Their practical significance comes from the fact that they can isolate a single risk, reshape a payoff, or express a view with far less capital than a direct cash position would require, while also introducing dependencies that are easy to underestimate. That dual character is what makes derivatives indispensable to many sophisticated portfolios and equally capable of magnifying errors in judgment, model assumptions, or execution.

Core derivative instruments and how they differ

The most basic distinction among derivative instruments is not complexity, but the nature of the claim they create. A forward or futures contract is a linear instrument: one party gains dollar-for-dollar as the underlying rises, and the other loses dollar-for-dollar. That makes the contract efficient for transferring price exposure, but it also means the economic consequences of a move in the underlying are unbounded on both sides. An option, by contrast, creates an asymmetric claim. The buyer pays a premium for the right, not the obligation, to act later, which introduces convexity and caps downside at the cost of giving up some or all of the premium. Swaps occupy a different space altogether: they are agreements to exchange cash flow streams, usually to transform the character of an asset or liability rather than to create a directional bet in the purest sense. Credit derivatives then add another layer, separating the risk of default or spread widening from the ownership of the underlying obligation itself.

That structural difference matters because each instrument answers a different portfolio problem. A futures contract is often the cleanest tool when the objective is to lock in a price, reduce basis risk, or express a view with high capital efficiency and transparent mark-to-market accounting. A forward serves a similar economic purpose, but its bilateral, customized nature makes it more suitable when the exposure is specific and the terms must be tailored. Options are used when the investor wants to define risk in advance, preserve upside, or monetize a belief about volatility rather than just direction. Swaps are preferred when the exposure is embedded in financing, funding, or asset-liability management, such as converting fixed-rate debt to floating or swapping one currency cash flow for another. Credit default swaps isolate credit events and spread risk, allowing institutions to hedge or express views on solvency and credit quality without transacting in the bond itself.

These instruments also differ in how they distribute risk through time. Futures and forwards are path-sensitive only through margining or counterparty exposure; their payoff at maturity is determined by the final relationship between contract price and market price. Options are path-dependent in a more meaningful economic sense because volatility, time decay, and the evolution of the underlying all interact to shape value before expiry. Swaps typically convert one set of periodic obligations into another, so their risk is tied to the term structure of rates, spreads, or foreign exchange rather than to a single terminal payoff. For a risk manager, that means the same notional amount can represent very different exposures depending on whether the contract is linear, optional, or cash-flow based. Notional alone is not a sufficient measure of economic risk.

Settlement mechanics further separate the instruments in practice. Exchange-traded futures and many listed options are standardized, centrally cleared, and marked to market, which reduces bilateral credit exposure but introduces variation margin and liquidity demands. OTC forwards, swaps, and bespoke options can be structured to match a precise exposure, but the customization comes with documentation, collateral, and counterparty considerations that can dominate the economics in stressed markets. The distinction is not merely operational. A contract that is easy to value in theory may still be expensive to carry if margin calls arrive during a drawdown or if the dealer relationship becomes a binding constraint. In that sense, the "best" derivative is often the one whose legal and funding structure fits the investor's balance sheet as well as the market view.

Options deserve special attention because they are the most explicit expression of nonlinearity in the standard derivatives toolkit. A call and a put are not just opposite directional views; they are different ways of paying for exposure to uncertainty. The premium represents the market's price for convexity, and that convexity can be used to limit loss, create leverage with defined risk, or shape a payoff around a specific event. The same feature that makes options attractive also makes them sensitive to implied volatility, time decay, and changes in distributional expectations. In contrast, a futures position is dominated by directional exposure and financing effects, with little built-in protection against adverse movement. A trader choosing between them is not just choosing a bullish or bearish expression, but deciding whether the strategy should be linear or nonlinear in the underlying.

Credit derivatives are often treated as a separate category because the underlying "asset" is not a stock, rate, or commodity price but a reference entity's credit quality. A default swap transfers default risk and spread risk while leaving ownership of the bond or loan untouched, which makes it useful for hedging concentrated credit exposure or separating credit views from funding decisions. This separation can be powerful, but it also highlights an important principle across the derivative universe: the contract may isolate one risk while leaving others intact. A hedge that removes price risk may still leave basis risk, liquidity risk, funding risk, or counterparty risk. The instrument is only as precise as the exposure it actually transfers.

The practical comparison, then, is not between "simple" and "advanced" derivatives, but between different forms of exposure transformation. Linear contracts transfer price risk directly. Optional contracts purchase asymmetry and convexity. Swaps transform the cash-flow profile of an existing balance sheet. Credit derivatives isolate default and spread risk. Once that taxonomy is clear, the choice of instrument becomes a design problem: what risk needs to be moved, what residual risks are acceptable, and what market structure can support the position when conditions are no longer benign. That framing is more useful than any attempt to rank instruments by sophistication, because sophistication in derivatives is usually just specificity about which risk is being paid to remove, retain, or amplify.

Who uses derivatives and why they matter in modern portfolios

Derivatives matter in modern portfolios because they let different institutions solve different problems with the same contractual toolkit. A pension fund may use futures to adjust equity exposure without disrupting a long-term allocation. An asset manager may use options to cap downside while preserving most of the upside. A commodity producer may use forwards to stabilize cash flow. A bank or dealer may use swaps to transform funding, duration, or currency exposure. The common thread is not speculation for its own sake, but the deliberate shaping of risk so that a portfolio can better match objectives, constraints, and liabilities.

That functional role is especially important because many portfolios are not built from a blank slate. They are already carrying embedded exposures from business lines, benchmark mandates, balance sheet structure, or policy constraints. Derivatives allow those exposures to be separated, modified, or offset without forcing the liquidation of core holdings. In practice, this means a manager can keep the desired asset base intact while using listed or OTC contracts to fine-tune beta, duration, convexity, volatility, or currency risk. The derivative becomes a control layer above the cash portfolio, not merely an additional position beside it.

For institutional investors, the appeal is often precision. Cash markets can be blunt instruments when the objective is narrow. If a portfolio needs temporary downside protection ahead of a catalyst, an index put spread may be more efficient than selling the underlying basket and later rebuilding it. If a liability-sensitive portfolio needs a duration adjustment, interest rate futures can provide immediate exposure with less balance-sheet disruption than trading the underlying bonds. If a global portfolio has foreign revenue or asset exposure, currency derivatives can isolate the translation risk that otherwise obscures performance. Derivatives are therefore central to portfolio engineering because they permit targeted adjustments with a level of granularity that cash instruments often cannot match.

They also matter because modern portfolio management is increasingly defined by uncertainty rather than static allocation. Return forecasts are noisy, correlations shift, and market regimes change. Research on empirical asset pricing has shown that more adaptive forecasting methods can materially improve investment decisions relative to simpler linear approaches [28], which reinforces the need for instruments that can be adjusted quickly as views change. Derivatives provide that adaptability. They allow a portfolio to express conditional views, hedge scenario-specific risks, and reallocate risk budget without waiting for full turnover in the underlying holdings.

Another reason derivatives are indispensable is that portfolios are judged not only by return, but by path. Two strategies with similar long-run expected returns can produce very different investor outcomes if one experiences deeper drawdowns, more frequent liquidity needs, or larger tail losses. Options, variance-linked positions, and structured overlays can reshape that path by introducing convexity or by transferring risk to parties willing to bear it. This is particularly relevant in environments where market behavior departs from the clean assumptions of textbook equilibrium. Behavioral and empirical work has long shown that prices can diverge from simple rational models and that investor expectations are shaped by more than fundamentals alone [29][31]. Derivatives give professionals tools to manage portfolios in that imperfect world rather than in an idealized one.

Risk managers use derivatives for the same reason they use limits, reserves, and stress tests: to make downside measurable and survivable. A portfolio that is nominally diversified can still be exposed to concentrated shocks if correlations rise in a crisis, if funding conditions tighten, or if volatility gaps higher. Historical episodes of liquidity stress and contagion show how quickly losses can spread once market participants are forced to delever or unwind hedges under pressure [4][8][34]. Derivatives can either mitigate or amplify those dynamics depending on how they are used, which is why they are central to both risk reduction and risk transmission. In a well-designed framework, they serve as shock absorbers; in a poorly governed one, they can become accelerants.

They also matter because some exposures are not conveniently available in cash form at all. Inflation risk, mortality risk, commodity basis risk, and cross-asset correlation risk are all examples of factors that may be economically important but difficult to manage directly through spot transactions. The growth of derivatives markets has been driven in part by the need to transfer these specialized risks to counterparties better positioned to warehouse them [33]. That transfer function is what makes derivatives so useful to insurers, pensions, energy firms, exporters, importers, and multi-asset allocators alike. They are not merely trading vehicles; they are mechanisms for aligning economic exposure with institutional purpose.

At the same time, the very flexibility that makes derivatives valuable also makes governance essential. Their effects are often nonlinear, their financing terms can change under stress, and their mark-to-market behavior can create liquidity demands long before the underlying thesis is proven right. This is why derivatives are rarely evaluated in isolation by sophisticated users. They are judged in context: how they alter portfolio variance, how they behave under stress, how they interact with margin and collateral, and whether they improve the risk-adjusted profile of the whole book. In modern portfolios, derivatives matter not because they are exotic, but because they make risk itself tradable, measurable, and, when used well, more controllable.

How leverage, convexity, and flexibility create opportunity and risk

Leverage is the first reason derivatives matter, but it is also the first reason they can fail. A small premium, margin deposit, or collateral posting can control a much larger notional exposure, which means the return on committed capital can be amplified dramatically. That amplification is not inherently good or bad; it simply concentrates the economic consequences of price movement into a smaller base. In a favorable move, leverage can make a modest directional view economically meaningful. In an unfavorable move, the same structure can turn a tolerable forecast error into a material loss, a margin call, or forced liquidation. The danger is not only the size of the exposure, but the speed with which the exposure can reprice when the market moves through a range that was assumed to be unlikely.

Convexity is what separates an option from a linear hedge or speculative forward. A linear instrument changes value in direct proportion to the underlying, while an option's value changes in a curved way because the payoff is contingent. That curvature creates asymmetry: the holder can participate in favorable moves without taking on the same magnitude of downside, at least beyond the premium paid. This is why options are so useful for expressing views with controlled loss, for insuring portfolios against abrupt declines, and for structuring payoffs around discrete events. But convexity is not free. The market charges for it through premium, implied volatility, and time decay. If the expected move does not arrive soon enough, or if realized movement is smaller than implied, the convexity that looked protective or attractive in theory can become an expensive drag in practice.

Flexibility is the third source of opportunity. Derivatives allow the investor to separate direction, time horizon, volatility, and financing considerations in ways that cash instruments usually do not. A portfolio manager can express a short-term view without disturbing a long-term allocation, hedge a single risk factor while leaving other exposures intact, or tailor a payoff to a liability profile rather than to a benchmark alone. That adaptability is especially valuable when the underlying cash position is costly to trade, operationally difficult to alter, or strategically important to retain. In that sense, derivatives are not merely instruments for speculation; they are tools for engineering exposure. The same flexibility also enables more subtle forms of risk transfer, including the shifting of risk into structures that appear benign until their embedded conditions are tested.

The interaction among these three features is where many sophisticated mistakes originate. Leverage magnifies outcomes, convexity makes those outcomes nonlinear, and flexibility encourages the belief that every risk can be surgically isolated. In reality, the risks tend to reappear in different forms. A hedged position may still be exposed to basis risk, volatility changes, term structure shifts, or correlations breaking down. An option position that seems defined-risk may carry meaningful path dependency if the underlying approaches the strike in a volatile market. A spread that reduces premium outlay may also reduce the margin for error if both legs respond differently to changes in implied volatility or liquidity. The more elegant the structure, the more important it becomes to ask which variables are truly neutralized and which are merely displaced.

This is why experienced users treat leverage and convexity as portfolio design variables rather than as abstract features of a contract. The question is not whether a strategy has upside, but what kind of upside it has, what must happen for that upside to be realized, and what hidden financing or rebalancing demands accompany it. A position can look conservative because its maximum loss is known, yet still be dangerous if the probability of that loss is high or if the path to that loss creates liquidity stress. Another position can appear aggressive because it uses little capital, yet be quite disciplined if its losses are limited and its convexity is purchased deliberately as insurance against a specific risk. The economic meaning of the trade depends on the distribution of outcomes, not on the nominal size of the position alone.

The market also tends to reward flexibility unevenly. When volatility is cheap and liquidity is abundant, optionality can be acquired at a relatively low cost, and investors are tempted to overuse it. When stress arrives, the same optionality can become expensive to roll, difficult to hedge, or impossible to monetize at the quoted price. This asymmetry is one reason complexity itself has become a concern in financial markets; structures that are easy to assemble can be much harder to unwind, explain, or supervise when conditions deteriorate [38]. For institutional users, the relevant discipline is not simply to identify attractive convexity, but to understand how the position behaves under adverse funding conditions, wider bid-ask spreads, and changing collateral demands.

The practical implication is that leverage, convexity, and flexibility should be evaluated together. Leverage determines how much exposure is embedded per unit of capital. Convexity determines whether the payoff accelerates or decelerates as the market moves. Flexibility determines whether the exposure can be adjusted without destroying the original economic thesis. Used carefully, the combination allows investors to shape risk with unusual precision, align portfolios with liabilities, and express nuanced views more efficiently than cash markets permit. Used carelessly, it creates positions that are easy to initiate, difficult to monitor, and even harder to exit once the market begins to test the assumptions that made them attractive in the first place.

Market structure, liquidity, and the role of exchanges versus OTC markets

Market structure determines whether a derivative is merely well priced on paper or actually usable in size. In listed markets, the exchange provides a standardized contract, a central rulebook, transparent quotes, and a clearinghouse that stands between buyer and seller. That architecture matters because it reduces bilateral credit concerns and makes the contract easier to value, hedge, and transfer. For many institutional users, the practical advantage is not just convenience; it is the ability to enter and exit positions with a clearer sense of execution quality, margin requirements, and counterparty exposure. The exchange does not eliminate risk, but it concentrates and formalizes it in a way that is often easier to govern.

Liquidity is the second layer of the problem, and it is more subtle than simple trading volume. A market can appear active while still being fragile if depth is thin, if quotes are unstable, or if liquidity vanishes beyond the best bid and offer. For derivatives, this fragility can be magnified by leverage and by the need to hedge dynamically. A dealer or trader may be able to transact at the screen price in small size, yet face a very different reality when trying to roll a large position, unwind a spread, or hedge a sudden delta change. In stressed conditions, the cost of immediacy rises quickly, and the apparent precision of pricing can give way to wide bid-ask spreads, partial fills, and execution slippage. Empirical work on illiquidity and serial correlation in hedge fund returns underscores how return patterns can be distorted when positions cannot be marked or traded cleanly [3].

Exchange-traded derivatives are designed to make liquidity visible. Open interest, volume, quote width, and expiry distribution all provide clues about how easily risk can be transferred. Yet even in listed markets, liquidity is not uniform across strikes, maturities, and underlyings. Near-the-money contracts in heavily followed indexes may trade with great efficiency, while deep out-of-the-money options or longer-dated contracts can be meaningfully less liquid. That unevenness matters because the contract that best matches a risk may not be the contract that is easiest to trade. Sophisticated users therefore think in terms of liquidity tiers: what can be traded immediately, what can be traded with patience, and what should perhaps be hedged indirectly through a more liquid proxy. The market may quote a theoretical price for every contract, but the executable price is what governs real portfolio outcomes.

Over-the-counter markets solve a different set of problems. OTC derivatives allow customization of notional size, maturity, underlying reference, embedded optionality, settlement terms, and collateral arrangements. That flexibility is indispensable when the exposure itself is bespoke, as in long-dated rate structures, tailored commodity hedges, or cross-currency risk that does not fit standard exchange contracts. But customization comes at a cost: pricing is less transparent, liquidity is less standardized, and the trader must manage counterparty credit, documentation, and collateral mechanics directly. In OTC markets, the trade is not just a price agreement; it is a negotiated relationship. The value of that relationship can be substantial, especially when the instrument must match a real-world exposure closely, but it also creates dependence on the dealer's balance sheet and willingness to intermediate.

This dependence became especially visible when dealer balance sheets were impaired. Markets can function smoothly when intermediaries are willing and able to warehouse risk, but they can seize up when financing becomes scarce or when dealers retrench. Research on dealer-bank failures shows how market intermediation itself can become a source of vulnerability [48], and broader evidence on intermediary asset pricing indicates that the pricing of many assets is shaped by the constraints of the institutions standing between buyers and sellers [45]. In practice, that means OTC liquidity is often contingent rather than unconditional. A quote is only as good as the dealer's capacity to honor it, and a hedge is only as good as the market's ability to absorb the offsetting flow when conditions deteriorate.

The exchange-versus-OTC distinction is therefore not a binary of good versus bad design. It is a tradeoff between standardization and customization, transparency and flexibility, central clearing and bilateral negotiation. Exchanges typically offer better price discovery, easier comparison across participants, and a more robust framework for margining and default management. OTC structures, by contrast, allow the contract to be built around the exposure rather than forcing the exposure into the contract. In many institutional settings, the best answer is a combination of both: use listed instruments where liquidity and transparency are paramount, and use OTC instruments where the risk is too specific to be captured cleanly by a standardized contract.

That combination also affects risk management at the portfolio level. A position that looks efficient in isolation may create hidden liquidity demands when aggregated with other exposures. A fund can be long liquidity in one book and short liquidity in another without realizing it until stress reveals the correlation. During calm periods, the difference between listed and OTC may seem operational; during stress, it becomes economic. Margin calls, collateral disputes, and widening dealer spreads can force otherwise sound positions into unfavorable liquidation. The investor who understands market structure is not merely choosing a venue. He or she is choosing how much of the trade's risk will be borne by the market, how much by the intermediary, and how much by the portfolio itself when liquidity is no longer abundant.

CHAPTER 2

Chapter 2: Options Fundamentals for Advanced Practitioners

With the broader market context established, the next step is to work from the contract itself, because option analysis begins with the legal and economic logic embedded in the payoff. For advanced practitioners, the essential task is not memorizing a definition but understanding how a relatively small set of contractual features produces a wide range of exposures, from simple directional bets to finely tuned risk transfers. That requires a disciplined reading of what the buyer receives, what the seller assumes, and how the contract behaves across different price paths, time horizons, and settlement conventions.

Calls, puts, and the logic of option payoffs

The payoff logic of options is easiest to understand by stripping away pricing, volatility, and market opinion and focusing on the contract's terminal state. A call gives its holder the right, but not the obligation, to buy the underlying at the strike price. That means the call buyer is participating in upside only after the market has moved far enough to overcome the strike and the premium paid. If the underlying finishes below the strike, the call expires worthless; if it finishes above the strike, the payoff rises dollar-for-dollar with further gains. The call's value at expiration is therefore $\max(S - K, 0)$, where S is the underlying price and K is the strike. The economic meaning is simple: the buyer has purchased convexity, paying a known amount today for a non-linear claim on future price appreciation.

A put is the mirror image in legal form, but not in economic effect. The holder has the right, but not the obligation, to sell the underlying at the strike price. At expiration, the put's value is max(K - S, 0). The put buyer benefits when the underlying falls below the strike, and the payoff increases as the market declines further. This is why puts are often used not only as speculative downside expressions but also as insurance instruments: they convert a falling market into a bounded, predefined claim. In portfolio terms, the put is the cleanest way to buy downside convexity without having to liquidate the asset itself. That feature matters because the risk being transferred is not merely price direction, but the asymmetry of losses relative to gains.

These terminal payoffs are deceptively simple, yet they generate the entire logic of option strategy design. A long call has limited downside equal to the premium and theoretically unlimited upside. A long put has limited downside equal to the premium and substantial upside as the underlying approaches zero. The seller of each option inherits the opposite profile: the call writer collects premium but faces open-ended upside risk, while the put writer collects premium but can be exposed to substantial losses if the underlying collapses. What looks like a small premium is therefore not a small risk transfer; it is a contract that redistributes tail outcomes. The asymmetry is the point. Option markets exist because some participants want to pay to cap risk, while others are willing to receive premium in exchange for bearing that risk.

The shape of the payoff is best understood by separating the strike from the premium. The strike determines where the contract begins to matter; the premium determines the cost of acquiring the right. A call bought for a premium of 4 with a strike of 100 does not begin to produce net profit until the underlying is above 104 at expiration. A put bought for 3 with a strike of 80 does not begin to produce net profit until the underlying is below 77. This distinction between gross payoff and net profit is essential in practice, because many errors in option analysis come from confusing the contract's intrinsic terminal value with the investor's actual economic result after paying for the exposure. The premium is not a footnote; it is the price of convexity and the hurdle that the market imposes for access to nonlinearity.

From the seller's perspective, the logic is equally important. The writer of a call or put is not simply "short an option"; the writer is short a contingent obligation whose probability and severity depend on the underlying distribution, time to expiration, and volatility regime. The premium received is compensation for assuming that obligation, but the compensation is not linear with risk. A short option position may appear attractive because most expirations end without dramatic movement, yet the payoff is structurally exposed to rare but large moves. This is one reason option selling requires more than a view on direction. It requires a view on the distribution of outcomes, the liquidity available to manage adverse moves, and the capital needed to survive periods when the market reprices tail risk abruptly. Work on market risk premia and option-implied information has shown that option prices embed expectations about return dispersion and crisis states, not just point forecasts [58].

The payoff diagram also reveals why calls and puts are the building blocks for more elaborate structures. Once the investor understands that a call is a piecewise-linear claim with a kink at the strike, it becomes straightforward to combine multiple strikes into spreads, collars, butterflies, and condors. Each structure is an engineered modification of the same basic geometry: one leg defines where exposure begins, another leg defines where it is capped, and the net position determines how much convexity is retained or sold. Put-call parity further links the two instruments through the relationship between the underlying, strike, rates, and dividends, showing that calls and puts are not isolated products but connected expressions of the same forward-looking valuation framework. The practical implication is that pricing and strategy design are inseparable from payoff algebra.

That algebra is also what makes options useful in markets where the distribution of returns is not well captured by a single average outcome. Equity markets, currency markets, and commodity markets all exhibit periods in which realized moves differ materially from what a simple linear model would suggest. The option payoff translates those distributional concerns into contract form. A call expresses a willingness to pay for upside participation; a put expresses a willingness to pay for protection or directional downside exposure. In both cases, the buyer is not predicting a single future price so much as purchasing a shape of exposure. The market, for its part, is continuously pricing that shape based on the collective assessment of volatility, skew, and the likelihood of extreme outcomes.

Intrinsic value, time value, and the forces behind premium decay

Option premium is not a single quantity so much as a layered price. The intrinsic value is the immediately exercisable portion of the contract: what the option would be worth if it expired right now, with no time remaining and no change in the underlying. For a call, that is the amount by which the underlying exceeds the strike; for a put, it is the amount by which the strike exceeds the underlying. If that amount is negative, intrinsic value is zero. Everything else in the premium is time value, which is the market's payment for the possibility that the option may become more valuable before expiration. That distinction is central because it separates what is already there from what is merely possible.

Time value exists because optionality has economic worth even when the contract is out of the money. A distant expiration gives the holder more chances for the underlying to move favorably, more opportunity for volatility to express itself, and more flexibility to wait for a better outcome. That flexibility is especially valuable when the distribution of future prices is wide, when a catalyst is approaching, or when the underlying can gap rather than drift. In practical terms, the market is not paying only for direction; it is paying for convexity, uncertainty, and the right to defer a decision. This is why two options with the same strike can trade at very different premiums depending on expiration, realized volatility expectations, and event risk.

Premium decay is the gradual erosion of that time value as expiration approaches. The passage of time is not neutral for an option buyer; it is a structural headwind. All else equal, the option loses the value of remaining uncertainty as there is less time for a favorable move to occur. This decay is not linear. It tends to accelerate as expiration nears, especially for at-the-money contracts, where the option's value is most sensitive to the remaining probability of finishing in the money. That acceleration is one reason short-dated options can appear deceptively inexpensive on a nominal basis while carrying substantial theta exposure on a daily basis.

The forces behind premium decay are not limited to the clock. Volatility is the most important companion variable. When implied volatility falls, the market is revising downward the expected range of future outcomes, and the time value component compresses accordingly. Even if the underlying price is unchanged, the option can lose value because the distribution of possible future prices has narrowed. Interest rates and dividends also matter, though their effect is usually more modest than volatility and time. Rates influence the carrying value of the strike payment and can shift call and put values in opposite directions;

dividends reduce the forward value of the underlying and therefore affect calls and puts asymmetrically. These inputs interact, but the practical message is simple: premium decay is the combined result of less time, less uncertainty, and changes in the economics of holding the underlying versus holding the right to transact in it.

For advanced practitioners, the useful question is not whether theta exists, but how it behaves across strike, maturity, and market regime. Deep in-the-money options often trade with relatively little time value because most of their price is already intrinsic, so their decay profile can resemble a financing adjustment more than a pure erosion of optionality. Far out-of-the-money options may carry low absolute premiums but still decay rapidly in percentage terms because their value is almost entirely time value. At the money, the option is most exposed to both gamma and theta: it can gain or lose value quickly because small changes in the underlying meaningfully alter the probability of finishing in the money. This is why short option positions can generate steady income in quiet markets yet become vulnerable when realized volatility increases or when the underlying begins to trend.

Market expectations also shape premium decay through the forward-looking nature of implied volatility. If participants anticipate an earnings announcement, policy decision, supply disruption, legal ruling, or macro release, the option may retain more time value than a simple calendar model would suggest because the market is pricing a discrete jump in uncertainty. Once that event passes, the premium can collapse even if the underlying move is modest, because the uncertainty that justified the elevated price has been removed. In this sense, premium decay is often event-driven rather than purely time-driven. The option holder is not only fighting the calendar; the holder is also fighting the market's continuous repricing of future uncertainty.

That is why option analysis must distinguish between price movement and decay mechanics. A long option can be correct on direction and still lose money if the move is too slow, too small, or too late. A short option can be profitable even if the underlying drifts modestly against the position, provided the decay of time value outweighs the adverse move. The premium is therefore a compact expression of forward expectations, and its decay reveals how those expectations are being consumed or revised. In practice, the trader who understands intrinsic value, time value, and the forces behind their decomposition is not merely reading a quote; the trader is reading the market's estimate of how much uncertainty remains, how quickly it is disappearing, and what price is being charged for the privilege of waiting.

Exercise styles, settlement methods, and contract specifications

Exercise style is the first contractual feature that determines how an option can be used in practice, because it defines when the holder may convert the option right into a transaction in the underlying. A European-style option may be exercised only at expiration, which keeps the payoff decision simple and pushes the holder's focus toward terminal value. An American-style option may be exercised at any time up to expiration, which adds flexibility but also introduces an early-exercise decision that depends on carry, dividends, financing rates, and the remaining time value in the contract. That distinction matters because early exercise is not merely a legal privilege; it is an economic choice. If the remaining time value exceeds the benefit of immediate exercise, the rational holder usually preserves the option rather than surrendering optionality too soon.

For equity options, early exercise is most relevant around dividends and deep intrinsic value. A call on a dividend-paying stock can become a candidate for early exercise when the dividend to be received by owning the shares exceeds the time value left in the option, adjusted for financing and transaction costs. A put can also be exercised early when the immediate receipt of strike proceeds is more valuable than keeping the option alive, especially when rates and borrow conditions make that cash flow attractive. In both cases, the analysis is not mechanical. The holder must compare the value of the optionality being abandoned with the economic benefit of taking delivery or cash now. This is why sophisticated desks do not treat American exercise as a mere feature of convenience; they treat it as a source of model and operational complexity, especially when dividend forecasts or borrow availability are uncertain.

Settlement method determines what actually changes hands when the option finishes in the money, and that distinction is often as important as the strike itself. Physical settlement requires delivery of the underlying asset or, in some contracts, a deliverable basket or futures position. Cash settlement replaces delivery with a monetary amount equal to the option's intrinsic value at expiration or exercise. Physical settlement is common when the underlying is easily transferable and market convention favors actual ownership transfer. Cash settlement is more common when physical delivery is impractical, when the reference asset is a broad index, or when the contract is designed to avoid delivery logistics. For index options, cash settlement is especially useful because the index is not itself deliverable; for single-name equity options, physical delivery is often the norm because the shares can be transferred directly.

The choice between physical and cash settlement changes hedging behavior before expiration. A physically settled option can force an exercise-and-delivery event that creates stock positions, borrow requirements, or financing needs. That can matter for desks managing large open interest near a strike, because pin risk and assignment risk become operational issues rather than purely theoretical ones. Cash-settled contracts reduce those delivery frictions, but they do not remove exposure; they simply convert the final value into cash at a specified reference price. In practice, settlement mechanics can influence liquidity, dealer positioning, and the behavior of traders who are trying to avoid or capture exercise-related flows near expiration. This is one reason price discovery in stocks and options is interdependent rather than one-way [77].

Contract specifications define the legal and economic geometry of the option. The underlying asset, strike increment, expiration cycle, contract multiplier, exercise style, settlement type, and trading calendar all affect how the instrument behaves. A standard equity option in the United States typically represents 100 shares, but the multiplier can differ for adjusted contracts, special corporate actions, or nonstandard deliverables. Strike spacing affects how finely a trader can tailor exposure, while expiration frequency affects the ability to roll or construct term structures. Minimum tick size and quote conventions influence transaction costs and the feasibility of precise hedges. Even seemingly small details, such as whether the contract is adjusted for a split, merger, or special dividend, can materially alter the economics of the position.

Contract specification also governs how derivatives interact with corporate events and market microstructure. When an issuer undergoes a split, spin-off, or extraordinary distribution, listed option contracts may be adjusted to preserve approximate economic equivalence. But "approximate" is the operative word: adjusted contracts can introduce odd strike levels, unusual deliverables, and reduced liquidity. That is why experienced traders examine the contract memorandum rather than relying on the ticker alone. In institutional settings, these details matter for risk systems, because the same nominal position can carry different exposures after an adjustment. The operational burden is not trivial; the operations-finance interface literature emphasizes that monetary exposures, information flows, and execution processes must be managed jointly under uncertainty [74].

Specification details also shape valuation and model behavior. A contract with early exercise rights, discrete dividends, or special settlement provisions may deviate from the assumptions embedded in the simplest pricing formulas. Empirical work has shown that pricing errors can widen in deeper out-of-the-money options and in higher-volatility environments, where model assumptions are more strained [82]. That does not mean the contract is mispriced in a casual sense; it means the trader must understand which contractual features are being approximated and where those approximations are likely to break down. In advanced practice, the option is never just "a call" or "a put." It is a bundle of rights, obligations, and specifications that determine how the payoff is realized, how the position is hedged, and how the contract behaves when market conditions become most difficult.

Reading option chains and interpreting market-implied expectations

An option chain is not just a list of strikes and premiums; it is a compressed map of how the market is currently distributing probability, uncertainty, and demand for protection across future price levels. The chain shows bids, offers, open interest, volume, and implied volatility for calls and puts at each strike and expiration. Read properly, it reveals where traders are paying up for convexity, where they are indifferent, and where they are structuring hedges around a specific event or price zone. The chain therefore functions as a live market survey, but one that must be interpreted with care. Prices in the chain reflect not only views on the underlying asset, but also inventory pressure, dealer hedging, skew preferences, funding costs, and the relative scarcity of contracts at different maturities.

The first layer of interpretation is the relationship between strike, expiration, and moneyness. Deep in-the-money options behave more like synthetic stock or bond exposure, while far out-of-the-money options often trade as cheap lottery-like convexity or tail insurance. At-the-money contracts usually carry the most time value and are the most sensitive to changes in implied volatility. The shape of the chain across strikes matters because it shows whether the market is assigning symmetrical uncertainty or leaning toward one side of the distribution. A steep put skew, for example, often indicates greater willingness to pay for downside protection than for upside participation. That does not automatically mean the market is predicting a decline; it may instead signal hedging demand from long-only portfolios, structured product desks, or participants who are already exposed to the underlying.

Implied volatility is the central language of the chain because it translates option prices into a common measure of expected movement. A higher implied volatility does not mean the market expects a larger realized move with certainty; it means traders are willing to pay a richer premium for optionality, whether because they anticipate turbulence or because they need insurance against it. Comparing implied volatility across strikes produces the volatility smile or skew, and comparing it across expirations produces the term structure. These surfaces are often more informative than a single quoted premium because they show where uncertainty is concentrated. Research on volatility measurement and forecasting has long emphasized that volatility is dynamic, clustered, and only partially predictable [83][85][87]. The option chain reflects that reality in market prices, not in hindsight.

A useful reading discipline is to separate what the chain implies about distribution from what it implies about positioning. Open interest and volume can reveal where the market has accumulated exposure, but they do not tell you whether that exposure is long or short without additional context. Large open interest at a strike may create a gravitational effect on the underlying near expiration if dealers are hedging those positions dynamically. In that sense, the chain can help identify potential pinning zones, acceleration points, or areas where gamma exposure may intensify intraday moves. Yet the same observed concentration can also be a sign of crowded hedges that may unwind abruptly if the underlying moves through the strike. The chain is therefore not a static forecast; it is a record of contingent flows that can change the market's own path.

Market-implied expectations are best inferred by comparing adjacent strikes and expirations rather than focusing on a single contract. The relative pricing of calls and puts at the same maturity can indicate whether downside insurance is expensive relative to upside speculation. The progression of premiums across expirations can show whether the market expects a near-term event or a more persistent regime shift. If front-month implied volatility is elevated while later maturities remain calmer, the chain is often pricing a discrete catalyst such as earnings, policy risk, inventory data, or a macro release. If longer-dated options are rich across many strikes, the market may be discounting a broader uncertainty regime rather than a single event. Stress-testing frameworks in finance are built on the same general idea: map the system under adverse scenarios rather than relying on one-point estimates [84]. Option chains do that continuously, but in market prices.

Interpreting the chain also requires awareness of how supply and demand distort the surface. A strike can look expensive because market participants want protection there, not because the underlying is objectively more likely to land there. Conversely, a seemingly cheap option may simply reflect weak demand, poor liquidity, or a contract that dealers are eager to sell because it offsets another book. This is why the chain should be read alongside bid-ask spreads, trade size, and changes in implied volatility after large prints. A contract that trades at a high implied volatility on little volume may be less informative than a slightly cheaper strike that absorbs repeated institutional interest. In liquid index options, the chain often reveals a sophisticated negotiation between hedgers and speculators; in less liquid names, it can be noisier and more vulnerable to stale quotes.

For advanced practitioners, the practical value of the chain lies in translating market prices into a probability-weighted view of future outcomes without mistaking that view for certainty. The chain can help identify where the market sees a fat tail, where it anticipates compression, and where it is charging the most for protection against a specific move. It can also expose inconsistencies: a strike may be priced as if a move is unlikely, while neighboring strikes imply a much wider distribution, suggesting a discontinuity in sentiment or market structure. Used well, the option chain becomes a diagnostic tool for volatility, positioning, and event risk. Used poorly, it tempts the trader to read too much into a single premium and too little into the full surface that produced it.

CHAPTER 3

Chapter 3: Pricing Theory and the Quantitative Engine

Pricing is where the option ceases to be a static contract and becomes a measured claim on an uncertain future. Once the payoff structure is understood, the next question is how the market assigns a present value to that uncertainty in a way that is internally consistent, tradeable, and hedgeable. That requires a shift from intuition about direction to a framework built around probability, replication, and the cost of carrying risk through time. The quantitative engine behind derivatives pricing does not eliminate judgment; it organizes it, translating market conditions into model inputs and model outputs into executable quotes.

Risk-neutral valuation and the intuition behind pricing models

Risk-neutral valuation is best understood as a pricing device, not as a statement about how investors actually feel about risk. In the real world, different market participants demand different compensation for bearing uncertainty, and those demands are embedded in the prices of stocks, rates, commodities, and options. The risk-neutral framework temporarily sets aside those heterogeneous preferences and replaces them with a synthetic probability measure under which every tradable asset, after discounting for carry, earns the risk-free rate. That change of measure does not claim that investors have become indifferent to risk; it simply creates a mathematically consistent environment in which the price of a derivative can be expressed as the discounted expected payoff under a measure that rules out arbitrage. The value of the framework is that it converts a difficult economic question—what should this contingent claim be worth today?—into a tractable pricing rule anchored in replication and no-arbitrage.

The intuition becomes clearer when the derivative is viewed as part of a hedged portfolio. If a payoff can be dynamically replicated with the underlying asset and cash, then its price cannot differ from the cost of that replication without creating a free lunch. In that sense, the option price is not derived from a forecast of where the market will likely end up; it is derived from the cost of carrying a position that reproduces the option's terminal cash flows. This is why the pricing model is so closely tied to hedging. A model that correctly describes how the option's value changes as the underlying moves allows the dealer or trader to offset risk incrementally, and the absence of arbitrage forces the option's present value to line up with that hedge. The theoretical elegance of the result is matched by its practical discipline: pricing and risk management are two sides of the same mechanism.

This is also why the risk-neutral probability distribution should not be confused with a forecast distribution. The market-implied distribution extracted from options reflects not only expected future states but also the compensation required for bearing those states, especially tail outcomes and jump risk. Option prices therefore contain information about the market's pricing of uncertainty, not merely its central expectation. Research on option-implied distributions has shown that these prices can be used to infer the market's risk aversion and the shape of the risk-neutral density [96]. For practitioners, that distinction matters because an option can be expensive even when the underlying move seems unlikely in a statistical sense, simply because the market places a high price on protection against that move.

The role of the risk-free rate in the model is often misunderstood as a mere discounting convention, but it is more structural than that. Once a derivative payoff is replicated or approximated by a self-financing strategy, the financing leg of the hedge must grow at the rate available to a default-free borrower or lender. That is what makes the pricing relation internally coherent. The model is not saying that all investors can borrow at the same rate in practice; it is saying that the no-arbitrage price is the one that would prevail in a frictionless market with a common financing benchmark. Real markets depart from that ideal through funding spreads, collateral terms, margin requirements, and balance-sheet constraints, but the risk-neutral framework remains the reference point from which those frictions are measured and adjusted.

Volatility enters the picture because the option's value depends not only on where the underlying may end up, but also on the path it may take to get there. A larger expected dispersion increases the value of convexity, even if the expected terminal price is unchanged. This is one reason volatility is treated as a primary state variable in pricing models and not as a secondary nuisance. Empirical work on volatility measurement and forecasting has repeatedly shown that volatility is persistent, time-varying, and often more informative for pricing than a simple historical average would suggest [83][85][87]. In practical terms, the market does not price an option as if volatility were constant and known; it prices the option as a claim on an uncertain distribution whose width, skew, and tail behavior are central to the premium.

That distributional emphasis explains why implied volatility is often more useful than a point estimate of future realized volatility. Implied volatility is the market's reverse-engineered answer to the question: what volatility input makes the model reproduce the observed option price? It is therefore a compact summary of the market's consensus, or disagreement, about future uncertainty. But even this summary must be interpreted carefully. The price of a put may embed not only expectations of downside movement but also demand for insurance, while the price of a call may reflect leverage demand, short-covering pressure, or event-driven speculation. Studies linking stock and option characteristics show that changes in call and put implied volatilities can carry cross-sectional information about future returns [97], which reinforces the point that option prices are not passive reflections of the underlying—they are active aggregates of demand, supply, and risk transfer.

For advanced users, the deeper intuition is that risk-neutral valuation is a language for translating uncertainty into tradable terms. It works because it ties price to a replicating strategy, but it remains informative because the resulting prices reveal where the market is willing to pay for asymmetry, insurance, and convexity. The model's assumptions are deliberately austere: frictionless trading, continuous rebalancing, and a stable relationship between the underlying and the derivative. Those assumptions are rarely exact in live markets, yet they provide a benchmark powerful enough to organize thinking, compare relative value, and identify where observed prices reflect genuine hedging demand rather than simple statistical expectation. In that sense, the risk-neutral measure is less a claim about the world than a disciplined way of reading it.

Volatility, interest rates, dividends, and time as pricing inputs

Once the contract structure is fixed, the remaining uncertainty in an option's value comes from a small set of inputs that the market continuously updates: the volatility of the underlying, the prevailing interest rate environment, expected dividends, and the time remaining until expiration. These are not independent in practice, but pricing models treat them as distinct channels through which the future is translated into today's premium. For advanced users, the point is not simply that these variables matter; it is that each one changes the shape of the distribution the option is exposed to, and therefore changes both the fair value and the hedge required to support that value.

Volatility is usually the dominant input because options are claims on variability, not just direction. Higher expected movement increases the probability that an option will finish in the money, and it also increases the value of convexity embedded in the contract. That is why implied volatility is often interpreted as the market's price for uncertainty rather than a direct forecast of realized movement. In practice, the market does not need to agree on a single statistical estimate of future variance for options to trade; it only needs a price at which buyers and sellers are willing to exchange exposure to that variance. The gap between implied and realized volatility is where many trading strategies begin, but it is also where many risk assumptions fail, because a volatility estimate that looks stable in one regime can reprice sharply when liquidity, macro conditions, or dealer positioning change.

Volatility also affects different strikes and expirations unevenly. A single "volatility" number is often too crude for actual trading, because the market expresses different views across the surface through skew and term structure. Deep out-of-the-money puts may carry elevated implied volatility because investors are willing to pay for crash protection, while nearer-term options may price event risk more aggressively than later maturities. This means that the option premium reflects not only the expected amplitude of price changes, but also the market's preference for protection at specific parts of the distribution. Empirical work on option-implied information shows that option prices can contain information about risk preferences and the shape of expected returns that is not visible in the underlying alone [101].

Interest rates enter the pricing problem through the time value of money and through the carry embedded in holding or deferring the underlying exposure. In a standard equity option framework, a higher risk-free rate generally raises call values and lowers put values, all else equal, because the strike payment is discounted and the present value of paying later becomes cheaper relative to paying now. The effect is usually smaller than volatility for short-dated equity options, but it becomes more relevant for longer-dated contracts and for instruments tied to rates, foreign exchange, or commodities where financing and carry are central to the economics of the trade. In rate-sensitive markets, the interest-rate assumption is not an abstract input; it is part of the underlying economics that the derivative is designed to transfer.

Dividends matter because they represent value that leaves the stock before expiration and therefore reduces the expected forward level available to the option holder. For calls, anticipated dividends are generally a headwind, since the stock price is expected to drop by the dividend amount on the ex-dividend date, lowering the probability that the call finishes in the money and reducing the expected terminal payoff. For puts, the same cash distribution tends to be supportive, because a lower expected forward level increases downside value. In practice, dividend assumptions are especially important around ex-dividend dates and for high-yield stocks, index options, and structured positions where the timing of cash flows can shift exercise incentives. Misestimating dividends is not merely a small input error; it can distort early-exercise decisions, parity relationships, and the economics of covered or synthetic positions.

Time is the input that binds all the others together. An option with more time remaining has a wider opportunity set in which volatility, rates, and dividends can express themselves, so time generally adds value even when the current spot price is unchanged. But time does not create value uniformly. The longer the horizon, the more opportunity there is for favorable movement, yet the more uncertainty accumulates about the path the underlying may take. That is why expiration is not just a calendar detail; it is a structural determinant of premium decay. Theta is the market's recognition that optionality is consumed as the contract approaches maturity, and the decay is not linear. Near expiration, small changes in spot or implied volatility can dominate the remaining time value, which is why short-dated options can behave like concentrated bets on micro-moves, event outcomes, or dealer flow.

The interaction among these inputs is what gives option pricing its practical complexity. A rise in volatility can offset the negative effect of time decay. A dividend expectation can alter the forward price enough to change which strike is most relevant. A shift in rates can matter more for one maturity than another. For this reason, professional pricing is less about plugging numbers into a formula than about understanding which input is likely to move, how that movement affects the surface, and how the resulting change propagates through a portfolio. Machine-learning methods have recently been used to improve the forecasting of asset risk premia and related cross-sectional patterns [28][102], but even sophisticated models do not remove the need to interpret the economic meaning of the inputs. They can sharpen estimates, yet the trader still has to decide whether the market is repricing uncertainty, carry, distributional shape, or simply temporary demand for protection.

That distinction matters because option prices are simultaneously a valuation output and a market signal. When implied volatility rises, the contract becomes more expensive not only because the mathematical fair value changes, but because the market is assigning a higher price to uncertainty itself. When rates or dividends shift, the forward level changes and the contract's terminal economics move with it. When time passes, the option loses optionality even if the underlying does nothing. The experienced practitioner treats these inputs as a linked system: volatility sets the breadth of possible outcomes, rates and dividends adjust the forward anchor, and time determines how long the contract has to realize its edge or expose its weakness.

Black-Scholes-Merton and extensions for real-market conditions

The Black-Scholes-Merton framework remains the central reference point for option pricing because it turns a difficult problem into a disciplined one: given a traded underlying, a financing rate, a dividend assumption, and an estimate of volatility, the model produces a unique theoretical price consistent with dynamic replication. Its power is not that markets literally obey its assumptions, but that it gives traders and risk managers a common language for translating uncertainty into a premium. The equation itself is now as much a market institution as a mathematical result, and its history shows how deeply a pricing formula can shape trading practice, hedging conventions, and even the way participants think about risk [24].

Under the standard assumptions, the option price is a function of the current underlying price, strike, time to expiration, risk-free rate, volatility, and dividends. The key insight is that the option's value can be replicated, at least in principle, by continuously adjusting a position in the underlying and cash. That replication logic is what makes the model so useful for relative value analysis and hedging. If the market price of the option differs materially from the model value, the trader is not merely seeing a misquoted contract; the trader is seeing a disagreement about the cost of carrying convexity through time. In practice, this difference is often where the trading edge begins, but it is also where model risk begins, because the input estimates are never perfectly observed.

Volatility is the most sensitive and most contested input. In the textbook formulation it is constant, but in live markets volatility is state dependent, clustered, and forward-looking. Empirical work has long shown that volatility changes over time in ways that are difficult to reconcile with a constant-variance assumption [7][83]. That is why practitioners treat Black-Scholes-Merton not as a literal description of the underlying process, but as a benchmark from which the market's implied volatility surface is inferred. The surface itself carries information about skew, term structure, and the market's valuation of downside protection. Option prices therefore encode more than expected variance; they embed the market's preferences, fears, and hedging pressure.

Once the model is used in real markets, the most common extension is not a single alternative formula but a family of corrections. Dividend-paying equities require an adjustment to expected carry. Index options often reflect discrete dividend assumptions rather than a smooth yield. American-style contracts may need early-exercise logic, especially for deep-in-the-money calls around dividend dates or puts when rates and carry make exercise economically rational. In rates and commodities, the relevant carry may not be a dividend at all but convenience yield, storage value, funding cost, or lease effects. These are not cosmetic changes. They alter the forward price embedded in the option and therefore change the boundary between intrinsic and time value.

Beyond carry adjustments, real-market pricing usually requires a more flexible volatility process. Stochastic volatility models allow variance itself to evolve randomly, which helps explain the observed persistence of skew and the fact that implied volatilities across strikes are rarely flat. Jump-diffusion models add discontinuous price moves, which matter when markets can gap on earnings, policy announcements, macro shocks, or supply disruptions. Local volatility frameworks fit the observed surface exactly at a point in time, while stochastic volatility models often do a better job capturing the dynamics of that surface through time. No extension is universally best. Each one is a trade-off between fit, tractability, and the intended use of the model, whether pricing, hedging, or scenario generation.

That trade-off becomes especially important when the model is used for risk rather than for quoting. A formula that prices today's option well may still produce unstable hedge ratios if its dynamics are poorly specified. A desk that relies on a constant-volatility assumption may appear well hedged in calm markets and then discover that the hedge breaks down precisely when volatility rises and correlations shift. For this reason, many institutional users calibrate the model to the implied surface rather than to historical returns alone, and then test the resulting prices against stress scenarios, alternative dynamics, and observed market behavior. Option-implied distributions can also be extracted from prices to reveal how the market is pricing tail risk and risk aversion, not just central tendency [96].

The practical value of Black-Scholes-Merton in advanced trading is therefore twofold. First, it provides a clean benchmark against which to measure relative richness or cheapness across strikes and expirations. Second, it serves as the base layer for extensions that acknowledge the frictions of actual markets: discrete dividends, early exercise, stochastic volatility, jumps, and non-flat term structures. Even where the assumptions are plainly violated, the model remains useful because deviations from it are informative. A surface that is steeply skewed, for example, tells a different story about crash demand than a flat surface would. A pricing model that ignores those deviations may still be mathematically elegant, but it will be economically incomplete.

Model limitations, calibration challenges, and parameter sensitivity

Pricing models are indispensable because they impose structure on an otherwise unbounded problem, but that structure is only as useful as the assumptions it can tolerate. The most common mistake in practice is to treat a model price as if it were a market fact rather than a conditional estimate. Every option model compresses reality: the underlying is assumed to evolve in a particular way, volatility is summarized by a small number of parameters, and the market is reduced to a finite set of tradable inputs. Those simplifications are not flaws in themselves; they are what make the problem tractable. The difficulty begins when the simplifications become invisible and the user forgets that the price is contingent on the model's internal logic, not independent of it.

Model limitations show up first in the gap between smooth theory and jagged market behavior. The canonical assumptions behind closed-form pricing are designed to permit replication and hedging, but actual markets feature jumps, discrete dividends, transaction costs, funding frictions, short-sale constraints, and liquidity that can vanish when it is needed most. A model may produce a clean value for a deep out-of-the-money option, yet the tradable market may embed a much richer set of concerns: crash risk, dealer inventory pressure, or demand for convexity from institutions that must protect against discontinuities. This is why two options with similar theoretical profiles can trade with very different implied volatilities. The market is not merely pricing the expected path of the underlying; it is also pricing the cost of carrying, hedging, and warehousing risk under real constraints.

Calibration is the process of forcing a model to speak the language of the market, but that process is rarely neutral. A model calibrated to the at-the-money surface may fit liquid strikes well and still perform poorly in the wings, where sparse quotes and wide spreads make the data noisier. A model built to match a single expiration may fail to preserve consistency across maturities. Even when the calibration objective is formalized as a least-squares fit to implied volatilities, the result can depend heavily on which strikes are included, how stale quotes are filtered, and whether the calibration is performed on mid prices, bid-ask averages, or executable levels. In practice, calibration is not simply about minimizing error; it is about deciding which errors matter most for the intended use of the model.

That issue becomes more pronounced when the model is used not just for pricing but for hedging and risk decomposition. A parameter set that reproduces market prices may still generate unstable Greeks, which is a serious problem for desks that rely on sensitivities to control exposure. Small changes in volatility, correlation, mean reversion, or jump intensity can produce materially different hedge ratios even when the headline price changes little. This is especially important in portfolios with nonlinear payoffs, where the shape of the surface matters more than any single point on it. The practitioner therefore has to judge a model on behavioral stability as much as on numerical fit: does it preserve sensible dynamics when inputs move, or does it create artificial jumps in exposure that cannot be managed in live trading?

Parameter sensitivity is the practical expression of model fragility. If a small change in an input produces a large change in output, the model may be mathematically elegant but operationally dangerous. Volatility is the most obvious example, because option value is often highly responsive to the assumed variance process. But the same concern applies to dividend assumptions, interest-rate curves, correlation structures, and any parameter that enters the payoff distribution indirectly. Sensitivity analysis should therefore be performed at two levels. The first asks how the option price changes when a parameter is perturbed. The second asks whether the calibration itself is stable under perturbation. A model that fits well only at a single point in parameter space may be overconfident by construction.

These issues are not merely technical; they are amplified by market structure and balance-sheet conditions. During periods of stress, the marginal price setter may be a constrained intermediary rather than a diversified, frictionless market participant, which changes the effective cost of risk transfer [108]. In such environments, the same model that worked during calm conditions can understate the premium demanded for convexity or overstate the ease of hedging a short option book. Regulatory and capital constraints can also affect risk appetite and market depth [6][92], which means calibration to a tranquil sample may embed a false sense of precision. For large institutions, the relevant question is often not whether the model is theoretically coherent, but whether it remains usable when funding costs rise, spreads widen, and balance sheets become scarce.

Robust practice therefore requires treating models as decision aids rather than truth engines. That means testing alternative specifications, comparing calibration windows, and examining whether the same trade thesis survives across reasonable parameter ranges. It also means distinguishing between fit and forecast: a model can match today's surface while still failing to anticipate how that surface will evolve under a new regime. Quantitative methods, including machine learning, can improve pattern recognition and parameter estimation, but they do not remove the need for economic discipline; they can just as easily amplify overfitting if the training data are narrow or the objective is poorly chosen [109][54]. In option markets, where payoffs are nonlinear and tail events matter disproportionately, robustness is often more valuable than marginal improvements in in-sample accuracy. The model that survives imperfect calibration and modest parameter drift is usually more useful than the model that looks optimal only at the point of estimation.

CHAPTER 4

Chapter 4: The Greeks, Sensitivities, and Dynamic Risk Control

Once the option price has been translated into a model, the trader's real problem shifts from valuation to exposure: how the position will respond as the market moves, time passes, and volatility changes. The Greeks provide that translation layer, turning a single premium into a map of conditional sensitivities that can be monitored, aggregated, and adjusted before small changes become large losses. For practitioners, this is where theory becomes operational, because a portfolio is rarely managed as a collection of isolated contracts; it is managed as a set of interacting risk factors whose combined behavior can differ sharply from the intuition attached to any one trade.

Delta, gamma, theta, vega, rho, and higher-order sensitivities

The first-order Greeks translate a position's price into a set of local response functions. Delta measures the immediate change in option value for a small move in the underlying; gamma measures how quickly that delta itself changes; theta captures the passage of time; vega measures sensitivity to volatility; and rho measures sensitivity to interest rates. These are not separate risks so much as different projections of the same contract onto the state variables that drive its value. A trader who focuses only on premium can miss the actual source of exposure, because two options with similar prices may behave very differently once the market begins to move. In practice, the Greeks are the bridge between pricing theory and risk control: they tell the desk what the position is doing now, not merely what it was worth at entry.

Delta is often treated as the most intuitive Greek because it approximates directional exposure. A long call typically has positive delta, a long put negative delta, and both approach the behavior of the underlying as they move deeper in the money. But delta is not a fixed characteristic of the contract; it is conditional on spot, strike, time to expiration, volatility, and rates. That conditionality matters because a delta-hedged book is only hedged at the moment of rebalancing. As the underlying moves, delta changes, and the hedge becomes stale. This is why practitioners speak of being “long” or “short” delta in a dynamic sense rather than as a permanent label. The relevant question is not whether a portfolio has delta, but whether the amount and sign of that delta are acceptable relative to the trader’s mandate, liquidity, and rebalancing tolerance.

Gamma is the Greek that explains why delta hedging is never free. Positive gamma means delta increases as the underlying rises and decreases as it falls; negative gamma means the opposite. For a long option holder, positive gamma is the source of convexity: the position gains directional responsiveness as the market moves in the favorable direction and loses responsiveness when it moves against it. For an option writer, negative gamma creates the familiar problem of having to buy into strength and sell into weakness when hedging. That rebalancing pattern can be manageable in calm markets, but it becomes expensive when realized volatility is high or when the underlying gaps across levels faster than the hedge can be adjusted. The practical implication is that gamma is not just a mathematical curvature term; it is a trading cost profile embedded in the position.

The interaction between gamma and theta is where many option books are won or lost. Long optionality usually carries negative theta, meaning time decay works against the holder if nothing else changes. Yet the same structure may be attractive if the trader expects enough movement, enough volatility, or enough convexity to offset that decay. Short option positions often collect theta, but they do so by absorbing the risk of adverse gamma. In other words, theta is the premium received for bearing the possibility that the market will move in a way that makes the hedge more difficult or more costly. This is why the apparent simplicity of "selling time decay" is deceptive: the income arrives slowly and predictably, while the losses can accelerate when the underlying starts to travel. The economics of the position are therefore best understood as an exchange between time carry and path dependence.

Vega introduces a different dimension of uncertainty: the market's valuation of future volatility. A position can be directionally neutral and still be highly exposed to changes in implied volatility. This matters because implied volatility is not merely a forecast; it is also a pricing variable that reflects supply, demand, event risk, and the market's willingness to pay for convexity. A long option position may benefit from a volatility expansion even if spot barely moves, while a short volatility position may suffer from a repricing of uncertainty even before any large price move occurs. In practice, vega risk is often concentrated around expirations, earnings dates, macro announcements, and regime shifts, when implied volatility can change more abruptly than the underlying itself. For that reason, volatility exposure must be managed as a separate line item, not as an afterthought to directional risk.

Rho is typically smaller than delta, gamma, theta, or vega for short-dated equity options, but it becomes more relevant when rates are meaningful, maturities are longer, or the underlying is rate-sensitive. A change in interest rates affects the present value of the strike, the carry embedded in the position, and the financing logic of replication. In rates and FX markets, rho can be central rather than peripheral, because the option's value is tied to the term structure of discounting and funding. Even in equity books, rho should not be dismissed automatically; it can matter when positions are long-dated or when the portfolio is being valued against a moving rate curve. The broader point is that rho reminds the trader that option pricing is not isolated from the funding environment in which the trade is carried.

Higher-order sensitivities become important when a portfolio is large, nonlinear, or exposed to regime change. Vanna measures how delta changes as volatility changes; charm measures how delta changes as time passes; vomma measures how vega changes as volatility changes; speed measures how gamma changes as the underlying moves. These second- and third-order effects matter because they explain why a hedge that is adequate under one market state can become unstable under another. In a concentrated book, the desk may be effectively long or short a combination of curvature, volatility convexity, and time decay that is not visible from the first-order Greeks alone. More advanced hedging frameworks therefore map not only the current sensitivities but also the sensitivities of those sensitivities, especially when the position is large enough that the hedge itself can move the market or when the underlying is prone to jumps and volatility clustering [120][122][124].

At the portfolio level, the challenge is not computing Greeks but interpreting them across instruments, expirations, and underlyings. A book that appears delta-neutral can still be structurally short gamma, long theta, and short vega, with each exposure behaving differently under stress. Aggregation across positions can also conceal offsetting risks that disappear when correlations break down or when the surface shifts nonuniformly. That is why sensitivity analysis is most useful when it is tied to scenarios: a parallel move in spot, a volatility shock, a rate shift, a time jump, and a gap event should all be tested against the same portfolio. In practice, the Greeks are most valuable when they are treated as a living risk map rather than a static report, because the market does not move one variable at a time, and neither does the portfolio.

Portfolio-level Greek aggregation and exposure mapping

At the portfolio level, Greeks are less like isolated option statistics and more like a translation system for the entire book. A desk may hold dozens or hundreds of positions across strikes, expirations, underlyings, and asset classes, yet the risk manager still needs a coherent answer to a simple question: what does this portfolio do if the market moves, time passes, volatility shifts, or correlations break? Aggregation is the process of reducing that complexity into a set of net sensitivities that can be monitored and controlled. But the reduction is only useful if it preserves the structure of the exposures that matter. A portfolio with a modest net delta can still carry substantial gamma, vega, or cross-asset convexity, and the apparent simplicity of the net number can conceal a highly nonlinear distribution of risk.

The first step is to recognize that Greek aggregation is conditional, not absolute. Delta, gamma, theta, and vega are usually computed locally around a current market state, so the aggregated portfolio Greek is itself a snapshot tied to a specific level of the underlying, implied volatility, rates, and time to expiration. That means the portfolio's profile changes as the market changes. A position that is nearly delta-neutral at one price may become directional after a small move because gamma has altered the hedge ratio. Likewise, a book that appears vega-balanced across nearby expirations may still be exposed to a term-structure shift if the options are clustered around one maturity bucket. For this reason, aggregation should never stop at a single net figure; it should be segmented by underlying, expiration, strike region, and risk factor so that the source of the exposure remains visible.

Exposure mapping extends aggregation by asking not only how much risk exists, but where it sits. A practical map organizes the portfolio by risk buckets: directional exposure to the underlying, convexity around key strikes, volatility sensitivity across the surface, and financing or carry sensitivity through time. In equity options, for example, the same net delta can arise from very different structures: a long call spread, a short put spread, or a combination of stock and options. Yet each structure produces a different path of losses and gains as the market moves. Mapping those differences is essential because two portfolios with identical headline Greeks may behave very differently under stress. One may be stable in small moves but vulnerable to a gap; another may be sensitive to a volatility repricing even if the underlying never trades far from spot.

The more nonlinear the book, the more important it is to aggregate Greeks across scenarios rather than rely on a single linear approximation. Nonlinear portfolios change character as the market moves through them. Gamma can flip the sign of delta exposure. Vega can concentrate in one part of the surface while disappearing in another. Theta can accelerate as expiration approaches, especially when the book is short optionality near the money. Sensitivity measurement for such portfolios is closely related to the broader risk-management literature on non-linear portfolios, where local approximations are useful but insufficient on their own [135]. In practice, this means the risk report should include not only current Greeks but also stressed Greeks under plausible shifts in price, volatility, and time decay. A book that is manageable in the current state may become materially different after a modest move in spot or a parallel shift in implied volatility.

Cross-greek effects matter as much as the primary measures. Delta aggregation tells you how the portfolio responds to the underlying, but it does not tell you how that delta will evolve as gamma works against or with you. Vega aggregation tells you how the book responds to volatility, but not whether that sensitivity is concentrated in short-dated options that will decay quickly or in long-dated structures that may dominate the risk budget for weeks. For institutional portfolios, exposure mapping should therefore separate where a risk resides from how it behaves. A commodity book, for instance, may have a small net delta to crude oil but meaningful exposure to the volatility of front-month contracts and the roll dynamics of the curve. A rates book may appear balanced in duration terms while still carrying substantial convexity around key strike levels in swaptions or caps and floors.

Aggregation also depends on the chosen unit of measure. Some teams report Greeks in contract terms, others in dollar terms, and still others in risk-equivalent units such as delta-adjusted notional or volatility points. The choice matters because it shapes the conversation between traders, risk managers, and senior decision-makers. A delta of 1,000 contracts means little without context; a dollar delta tied to a one-point move in the underlying is more interpretable, and a scenario-based map is more actionable still. The best reporting frameworks combine several views: a raw Greek summary for precision, a dollarized summary for comparability, and a scenario grid for intuition. This layered presentation is especially important when portfolios span multiple underlyings, because a single standardized metric can hide differences in contract size, multiplier, liquidity, and settlement conventions.

Exposure mapping becomes most valuable when it is linked to limits and governance. A risk system should not merely state that a portfolio has a certain delta or vega; it should indicate whether those exposures are concentrated near a few strikes, whether they are concentrated in a single expiration, and whether they are likely to expand under stress. That allows the desk to distinguish between manageable exposure and hidden fragility. It also supports more disciplined hedging, because the hedge can be chosen to offset the actual risk profile rather than the superficial net number. In that sense, Greek aggregation is not the end of risk measurement but the beginning of a usable map: one that shows how the portfolio is built, where it is vulnerable, and which market moves would change its character most quickly.

Hedging techniques for directional and volatility risk

Directional hedging begins with a simple question: what part of the position is actually being defended? If the risk is primarily a move in the underlying, the hedge should be built around delta exposure first, because delta is the component that most directly converts price change into mark-to-market change. A long equity book with positive delta can be partially offset with index futures, a put spread, or a collar depending on how much downside is being transferred and how much upside the holder is willing to surrender. The choice is not just about cost. Futures are efficient for reducing linear exposure, but they do not provide convexity. Options are more expensive in premium terms, yet they can preserve the portfolio's upside while defining the loss profile. In practice, the hedge is selected by matching the economic objective to the shape of the payoff, not by searching for the cheapest instrument in isolation.

For portfolios with concentrated single-name risk, the first layer of defense is often a direct offset in the same underlying or in a closely related proxy. When that is not feasible, practitioners move to cross-hedges, but the basis risk must be treated as a real exposure rather than a rounding error. An airline may hedge jet fuel with a crude-linked contract, an equity manager may hedge a sector basket with an index future, and a commodity merchant may hedge a physical position with a more liquid but imperfectly correlated contract. The hedge ratio should reflect the empirical relationship between the position and the hedge instrument, and that relationship should be monitored over time because correlations can weaken precisely when stress rises. This is one reason quantitative methods are increasingly used to estimate hedge effectiveness and update ratios dynamically rather than assuming a static mapping will remain stable [28][102].

Directional hedges also have to account for the fact that risk is rarely linear across the full range of outcomes. A position that is only modestly delta-exposed today can become far more sensitive after a large move because gamma changes the slope of the exposure. That is why a hedge that looks adequate at initiation may fail after a sharp rally or selloff. Dealers and active managers therefore distinguish between a static hedge, which is chosen once and left alone, and a dynamic hedge, which is adjusted as the market moves. Dynamic hedging can reduce directional risk more precisely, but it increases trading frequency, transaction costs, and the likelihood of execution slippage. The practical question is not whether to hedge delta, but how much rebalancing the portfolio can tolerate before the hedge itself becomes a source of instability.

Volatility hedging addresses a different problem: not the direction of the move, but the uncertainty around the move. A portfolio can be directionally neutral and still lose money if implied volatility rises against a short-volatility position or collapses against a long-volatility structure. The cleanest hedge for volatility risk is often another option position whose vega offsets the existing book, but vega is not a single scalar in real markets. It varies by strike, expiration, and skew exposure, so two positions with similar headline vega can behave very differently when the smile shifts. A short call book may be vulnerable to upside volatility, while a short put book may be more exposed to downside skew and crash convexity. Hedging that risk may require not just reducing aggregate vega, but reshaping the surface exposure with calendars, diagonals, or spreads that target the part of the volatility structure most relevant to the original book.

The distinction between implied and realized volatility is central here. A trader who is short premium is implicitly betting that realized movement will stay below the level embedded in option prices, while a long-volatility position is paying for the possibility that realized movement will exceed what the market has priced. Hedging volatility risk, then, is not simply about buying protection after the fact; it is about controlling the portfolio's exposure to the volatility regime itself. That may mean reducing short gamma into event risk, rolling short premium before liquidity thins, or pairing a directional view with a long-volatility overlay so that a sharp move does not overwhelm the thesis. In volatile markets, the cost of being wrong about volatility can exceed the cost of being wrong about direction because the hedge ratio itself becomes unstable as prices accelerate.

Effective hedging requires attention to the interaction between directional and volatility sensitivities, because they are often inseparable in practice. A long put may protect downside, but it also introduces negative theta and positive vega; if the market drifts sideways, the hedge decays even while it remains unused. A short call overlay may generate income, but it can cap upside and leave the portfolio exposed to a volatility expansion that makes the call more expensive to repurchase. For that reason, sophisticated hedging is usually framed in terms of risk budgets rather than single trades. The manager decides how much delta, gamma, and vega the portfolio can carry, then selects instruments that move those exposures toward the target while preserving the strategic intent of the book. This is where the portfolio view matters more than the trade-by-trade view: a hedge that looks elegant in isolation can be destructive if it concentrates risk elsewhere in the book.

Modern hedging practice increasingly relies on data-driven estimation of exposures and hedge effectiveness. Machine learning methods can be useful when the relevant relationships are nonlinear, unstable, or dependent on a wide set of market variables, and recent work shows that such methods can improve empirical forecasting and risk-premium estimation relative to simpler regression approaches [28][102]. That does not eliminate the need for judgment. A model can estimate that a hedge ratio should change, but it cannot decide whether a trader should accept basis risk, reduce gross exposure, or spend premium to buy convexity ahead of a known catalyst. Those decisions still depend on the portfolio's mandate, liquidity constraints, and tolerance for drawdown. Hedging, in that sense, is not the mechanical elimination of risk; it is the controlled reallocation of risk into forms that the institution is prepared to bear.

Managing gamma scalping, theta decay, and rebalancing discipline

Gamma scalping only works when the trader understands that gamma is not a profit source by itself; it is a curvature exposure that must be monetized through disciplined rebalancing. A position with positive gamma gains delta as the underlying rises and loses delta as it falls, which means the book becomes increasingly aligned with favorable moves and increasingly hedged against adverse ones. That sounds attractive, but the edge is fragile. The scalper is effectively buying low and selling high through repeated hedge adjustments, while paying the spread, commissions, and any slippage each time the hedge is changed. The strategy therefore depends on the realized path of the underlying, not just its final level. If the market moves in a choppy, mean-reverting way, the repeated adjustments can harvest incremental gains. If the market trends cleanly in one direction, the trader may be forced to chase the move and give back much of the convexity premium through rehedging costs.

That path dependence is why gamma scalping cannot be separated from theta decay. Positive gamma is usually financed by negative theta: the option portfolio loses time value as expiration approaches, and the trader must earn enough from realized volatility to offset that bleed. The practical question is not whether gamma is "good" and theta is "bad," but whether the realized volatility captured through hedge rebalancing exceeds the time decay and transaction costs embedded in the position. In that sense, gamma scalping is a volatility trade with a carry budget. When implied volatility is rich relative to the market's expected realized movement, the position may be too expensive to hold even if the directional view is neutral. When implied volatility is cheap and the underlying is likely to oscillate, the same structure can become attractive. The point is that the option premium is paying for the right to rebalance into convexity, and that right must be used efficiently.

Rebalancing discipline is what separates a controlled gamma book from an undisciplined one. The hedge should not be adjusted because the trader feels uneasy about a move; it should be adjusted because the portfolio's risk has crossed a predefined threshold. Those thresholds are often expressed in delta bands, underlying price intervals, or time-based intervals, but the logic is the same: reduce discretion and make the hedge rule-based. A trader who rehedges too frequently may turn a theoretically profitable structure into a frictional loss machine. A trader who rehedges too infrequently allows delta to drift so far that the position stops behaving like the intended volatility trade and starts behaving like an accidental directional bet. The discipline lies in choosing a hedge frequency that balances convexity capture against trading costs, market impact, and operational burden.

That balance becomes more delicate when liquidity thins or when the underlying becomes jumpy. In calm conditions, small hedge adjustments can be executed with minimal market impact, and the scaling of gains and losses remains relatively predictable. In stressed markets, spreads widen, quotes may disappear, and the hedge itself can become part of the problem. This is one reason that institutional risk management treats liquidity as part of the Greeks conversation rather than as a separate afterthought. A theoretically delta-neutral position can still be practically fragile if the underlying gaps through the rebalancing threshold faster than the desk can trade. The market history of liquidity shocks shows that the ability to hedge in size is often what determines whether a volatility position remains a managed exposure or becomes a forced liquidation [1][4].

For that reason, the trader must distinguish between continuous hedging as a model ideal and discrete hedging as a market reality. The idealized intuition assumes that delta can be neutralized at every infinitesimal price change, but actual desks operate with finite quote depth, execution delays, and transaction costs. The hedge ratio should therefore be linked to the instrument's liquidity, the size of the book, and the expected speed of the underlying's moves. A large index option position may support tighter rebalancing than an illiquid single-name or commodity option book. Likewise, a position with strong gamma near expiration may require more active management than one with longer tenor and slower sensitivity drift. The relevant issue is not merely the magnitude of gamma, but how quickly that gamma translates into changing delta relative to the market's ability to absorb trades.

There is also a conceptual risk in treating gamma scalping as a mechanical source of income. The strategy is often described in clean terms: buy gamma, sell delta into strength, buy delta into weakness, and capture volatility. But this description hides the fact that the trader is making a forecast about realized variance, the distribution of price paths, and the cost of implementation. In practice, the edge depends on whether the realized path produces enough two-way trading to overcome theta and execution drag. That is why sophisticated users often monitor the ratio of realized volatility to implied volatility, but do so with awareness that historical volatility alone is not a trading signal. A machine-learning forecast may improve the estimate of future risk premiums or realized variance, yet the execution problem remains separate: even a good forecast can be undermined by poor hedge timing or excessive turnover [28].

Discipline also means knowing when not to scalp. If the position's purpose is tail protection, the trader may accept theta decay as insurance cost rather than attempting to monetize every fluctuation. If the position is a volatility expression, the trader may decide that the hedge frequency should be reduced during illiquid hours or around scheduled events when gap risk dominates micro-movements. The same option book can therefore be managed under different regimes, but only if the desk is explicit about the objective. Gamma scalping is not a universal best practice; it is a technique suited to a specific combination of convexity, liquidity, and realized movement. The trader who respects that boundary is less likely to confuse a properly hedged volatility position with a disguised directional trade, and less likely to let small, repeated execution errors erode the very convexity the position was meant to capture.

CHAPTER 5

Chapter 5: Core Options Strategies for Market Conditions

With the contract mechanics and risk sensitivities already established, the next step is to translate that framework into position design. Options are not used in practice as isolated instruments for their own sake; they are assembled into structures that express a view on direction, income, volatility, or bounded risk under a specific market condition. The same underlying asset can support very different exposures depending on strike selection, expiration, premium outlay, and whether the trader is seeking participation, protection, or cash flow. That is why strategy selection is less about naming familiar trades than about matching payoff shape to the market environment and the portfolio's tolerance for adverse movement.

Directional strategies: long calls, long puts, and synthetic positions

Long calls are the cleanest expression of positive directional conviction in options, but their simplicity is easy to overstate. The buyer pays a finite premium for a claim on upside beyond the strike, and that premium defines both the maximum loss and the hurdle the underlying must clear before the position contributes economically. In practice, a long call is not just a bet on higher prices; it is a bet that the expected move, realized volatility, and timing of the move are sufficient to overcome the option's time decay and implied volatility level. That is why long calls are often most effective when the trader expects a discrete catalyst, a trend continuation, or a repricing event that can occur before expiration compresses the remaining extrinsic value. The appeal is convexity: downside is limited to the premium, while upside can expand with the underlying in a way that a cash-equity position cannot match on a dollar-for-dollar capital basis.

Yet the same convexity that makes long calls attractive also makes them fragile when the directional thesis is correct but late. A call can be "right" on market direction and still lose money if the move arrives after theta has done its work or if implied volatility was paid too richly at entry. For that reason, strike selection is not a cosmetic decision. Deep in-the-money calls behave more like leveraged stock replacement, with higher delta and lower time decay, while out-of-the-money calls offer cheaper convexity but require a larger move and are more exposed to the probability of expiring worthless. The choice between them is a choice about how much of the premium is being spent on immediate participation versus optionality. Experienced traders often think in terms of expected path rather than terminal price alone: the more front-loaded the move is expected to be, the more tolerable a shorter-dated, higher-gamma structure becomes.

Long puts mirror the long call's asymmetry, but their economic role is often broader than a simple bearish view. A long put can be a direct directional expression, a hedge against a concentrated long position, or a way to monetize a view that downside risk is underpriced relative to upside drift. Because equity indices and many risk assets exhibit negative skew, put demand often reflects not only opinion but also insurance behavior and portfolio defense. That makes puts especially sensitive to implied volatility, which is frequently elevated when markets are already uneasy. A trader buying puts in that environment is not merely paying for direction; the trader is paying for protection when protection is expensive. The position can still be justified if the expected loss avoided, the tail risk transferred, or the anticipated speed of decline outweighs the premium paid, but the decision should be made with explicit attention to carry cost and decay.

Long puts also behave differently across moneyness. A near-the-money put tends to carry substantial delta and meaningful gamma, making it responsive to incremental downside but also costly to hold. A far out-of-the-money put may be much cheaper and can serve as a tail hedge, but it may contribute little unless the market move is severe enough to push it into relevance. This distinction matters because not all bearish views are alike. A moderate pullback, an earnings miss, a policy shock, and a disorderly liquidation each justify different strike and maturity choices. The contract should be matched to the expected distribution of outcomes, not simply to the desire to be short. In institutional practice, that matching process is often more important than the outright bearish thesis itself, because the wrong put structure can consume carry without delivering protection when the book needs it most.

Synthetic positions extend the directional toolkit by separating economic exposure from the physical holding of the underlying. A synthetic long stock position can be created by buying a call and selling a put at the same strike and expiration; a synthetic short stock position reverses that combination. The payoff profile closely resembles the underlying, but the financing, margin, tax, borrowing, and execution characteristics can differ materially. This is why synthetics are not merely academic constructs. They are used when the trader wants equity-like exposure without purchasing shares, or when shorting the underlying is difficult, expensive, or operationally inconvenient. In some markets, the synthetic route can also improve capital efficiency or facilitate rapid exposure changes without disturbing existing holdings.

The practical value of synthetics is that they reveal when two exposures are economically similar but operationally distinct. A trader who is long a call and short a put at the same strike is effectively long the underlying, yet the position may carry different financing costs than stock ownership and may be subject to option-specific margin and assignment mechanics. Likewise, a synthetic short can substitute for a physical short sale when stock borrow is scarce or costly. But synthetics are not free of basis risk. Dividends, early exercise, borrow constraints, and changes in implied volatility can make the replication imperfect, especially as expiration approaches or as the underlying passes through the strike. The closer the position is to expiration, the more the details of exercise and settlement matter relative to the simple payoff diagram.

For advanced practitioners, the common thread across long calls, long puts, and synthetics is that direction is only one dimension of the trade. The other dimensions are financing, timing, carry, and implementation. A position can be bullish, bearish, or synthetic in structure, yet its real performance will still be shaped by the implied volatility paid or collected, the speed of the underlying move, and the desk's ability to manage the position before extrinsic value erodes. This is why directional option trades are rarely evaluated only on whether the market went up or down. They are evaluated on whether the chosen contract converted a view into a favorable risk-adjusted payoff under the actual path the market took.

Income strategies: covered calls, cash-secured puts, and spreads

Income-oriented option writing is often presented as a conservative alternative to outright speculation, but that label only makes sense if the trader is precise about what kind of income is being harvested and what risks are being sold in exchange. Covered calls, cash-secured puts, and vertical spreads all generate premium by transferring some combination of upside, downside, or volatility exposure to another party. The premium received is not free yield; it is compensation for assuming a contingent obligation whose value changes as the underlying, implied volatility, and time to expiration change. In practice, these structures are best understood as ways of reshaping the distribution of outcomes around an existing view on the underlying, not as substitutes for cash income.

A covered call combines a long position in the underlying with a short call against it. Economically, the writer is agreeing to deliver the underlying at the strike if assigned, while retaining the stock or futures exposure until that point. The premium lowers the cost basis and can improve return in flat or mildly rising markets, but it also caps upside beyond the strike. That cap is not a minor detail; it is the central trade-off. If the underlying rallies sharply, the short call offsets gains above the strike, and the strategy underperforms a simple long position. The structure therefore suits investors who are willing to exchange some convexity for premium and who already hold a view that the underlying is unlikely to make a large move in the near term.

The covered call's appeal is strongest when the trader has a clear framework for expected range, dividend timing, and implied volatility. Higher implied volatility makes call premium richer, which can improve the income profile, but it also indicates that the market expects larger movement, raising the probability that the call will be challenged or assigned. Dividend-paying stocks add another layer because call holders may exercise early when the remaining time value is small relative to the dividend, especially if the call is deep in the money. The writer must therefore treat assignment as a real operational outcome rather than a theoretical possibility. For institutional portfolios, the covered call can function as a systematic overlay, but the portfolio manager should still monitor ex-dividend dates, strike selection, and the interaction between premium collection and foregone upside.

A cash-secured put is the mirror image in economic intent: the trader sells a put and reserves enough cash or liquid collateral to buy the underlying if assigned. This structure expresses a willingness to own the asset at an effective entry price below the current market, while collecting premium in the meantime. The premium provides partial downside buffer, but only down to the extent of the collected credit. Below the strike, losses begin to accumulate in the same direction as a long position, reduced by the premium received. That makes the cash-secured put less a "safe income" trade than a conditional acquisition strategy. It is most defensible when the trader genuinely wants the underlying at a lower basis and is comfortable holding it through adverse price movement if assignment occurs.

The difference between a cash-secured put and an uncovered short put is not cosmetic; it is a capital and risk-management distinction. By reserving cash, the trader avoids forced liquidation and ensures the obligation can be met without relying on margin expansion or external financing. This matters because option premium can look attractive precisely when the market is paying for downside protection, and that is often when liquidity conditions are least forgiving. In stressed markets, the cost of rolling or closing short premium can rise quickly, and the cash reserve becomes part of the strategy's resilience rather than idle capital. The same logic that makes the structure appear conservative also explains why return on capital can be lower than more leveraged premium-selling approaches.

Spreads introduce a different income profile because they offset one option position with another, usually reducing both premium received and tail exposure. A credit spread, such as a short call spread or short put spread, collects net premium while defining the maximum loss by purchasing a farther out-of-the-money option. The result is a bounded-risk structure that sacrifices some income in exchange for known worst-case exposure. This is often preferable when the trader wants to monetize a view on range or probability without taking on the open-ended risk of a naked short option. In practical terms, the spread converts a pure volatility sale into a more controlled expression of conviction about where the underlying is unlikely to go.

The key analytical question for any spread is not whether it produces income, but whether the premium collected is adequate compensation for the probability-weighted loss profile after transaction costs, assignment risk, and slippage. Because the long leg limits disaster, credit spreads can look deceptively benign on a screen, especially when the maximum loss is far larger than the maximum gain. That asymmetry demands discipline in strike selection and position sizing. Traders often prefer spreads when they want a defined-risk substitute for naked premium selling, when margin efficiency matters, or when they need to express a directional view with a better capital footprint than outright stock ownership. But the strategy still depends on the same core variables as every option structure: distance from the money, time decay, implied volatility, and the path the underlying takes before expiration.

Across all three structures, the common mistake is to judge them by premium alone. Premium is only the starting point; the real question is what exposure has been sold to obtain it. Covered calls monetize upside cession, cash-secured puts monetize willingness to buy weakness, and spreads monetize a bounded probability view. Each can be appropriate in the right context, and each can become a disguised risk transfer if the trader confuses income generation with risk reduction. A disciplined practitioner evaluates these trades as contingent balance-sheet decisions: what capital is committed, what scenario produces the worst result, how liquid the position will be if the market gaps, and whether the premium earned is sufficient compensation for the path-dependent obligation assumed.

Volatility strategies: straddles, strangles, and calendar structures

Volatility strategies are built around a simple but often misunderstood proposition: the trader is not primarily forecasting direction, but the size, timing, and persistence of movement. A straddle and a strangle both express the view that realized movement will be large enough to overcome the premium paid, while a calendar structure expresses a different view altogether—that the term structure of volatility and the passage of time can be exploited by separating near-term and longer-dated exposure. In each case, the underlying asset matters less than the path it takes and the market's changing estimate of uncertainty along that path.

A long straddle combines a call and a put at the same strike and expiration. It is the most direct expression of a volatility view because the position benefits from a large move in either direction, provided the move is large enough to cover the total premium. The attraction is symmetry: the trader does not need to predict whether the move will be up or down, only that the market will travel far enough. The cost of that symmetry is time decay. If the underlying remains near the strike and implied volatility does not expand further, the position bleeds. That makes the straddle especially sensitive to the relationship between implied and realized volatility. If implied volatility is rich relative to the trader's expectation of actual movement, the position can be expensive even when the directional thesis is correct in a broad sense.

A strangle uses out-of-the-money call and put strikes instead of a single at-the-money strike. Economically, it is a cheaper way to buy convexity, but the trade-off is that the underlying must move farther before the position becomes meaningfully profitable. That lower entry cost can be useful when the trader expects a catalyst but wants to reduce premium outlay, or when the goal is to express a volatility view with a wider profit zone and a lower theta burden. The structure is common around earnings, policy announcements, litigation events, commodity inventory releases, or macro data that can reprice expectations abruptly. Yet the apparent efficiency of the strangle can be deceptive: because the strikes are farther from spot, the position may spend more time in a zone where it looks inexpensive but remains unproductive.

For both straddles and strangles, implied volatility is not just an input; it is part of the trade itself. A long volatility position is effectively a claim that the market is underpricing future movement or that uncertainty will rise enough to offset carry costs. Research on option returns has repeatedly shown that volatility risk is priced, particularly in index options, which helps explain why seemingly obvious long-volatility trades are not free money [147][148][151]. That means the trader must distinguish between buying volatility because it is cheap relative to expected realized movement and buying it because the position feels protective. Those are not the same decision. Protection may be justified even when the expected value is negative, but then the trade should be treated as insurance, not alpha.

Calendar structures change the problem by exploiting differences across expiration dates. A standard calendar spread buys the longer-dated option and sells the shorter-dated option at the same strike. The position is usually designed to benefit from faster decay in the front month than in the back month, while preserving exposure to a later move in the underlying. In effect, the trader is isolating the term structure of volatility and theta rather than making a pure directional bet. If near-term implied volatility is elevated relative to deferred volatility, the short leg can decay quickly; if the underlying remains near the strike into the front expiration, the spread may gain value as the short option loses time premium more rapidly than the long option.

This structure is especially useful when the market is expected to be temporarily overfocused on a near-term event while longer-dated uncertainty remains less disturbed. A calendar can also be adapted into diagonals by changing strikes, but the core logic remains the same: the trader is separating time horizons and monetizing the mismatch in how the market prices them. Unlike a straddle or strangle, which is usually a direct bet on realized movement, a calendar is often a relative-value trade on volatility term structure. That makes it more nuanced to manage, because the position can be helped by stable spot prices, but also by shifts in the volatility surface that are not obvious from the underlying alone.

Risk management for these structures begins with recognizing that they are path-dependent. A long straddle or strangle can lose value even if the market eventually moves, if the move arrives too late or after implied volatility has already collapsed. A calendar can be hurt if the underlying moves too far away from the short strike before the front option expires, because the short leg may stop decaying benignly and begin to dominate the spread's behavior. Gamma, theta, and vega are all active at once, but not in the same proportions across the life of the trade. The practical question is therefore not whether the structure is "bullish" or "bearish," but whether the trader has a credible view on realized movement, volatility level, and volatility timing.

That is why these strategies are often paired with event analysis, scenario mapping, and explicit exit rules. A volatility position that is entered because an event is expected to be large should be evaluated against the implied move already embedded in the option chain, the likely post-event vol crush, and the distance required for breakeven. A calendar should be evaluated against the shape of the term structure and the market's tendency to reprice near-term uncertainty faster than deferred uncertainty. In practice, the edge comes from understanding that volatility is not one number but a surface of expectations that changes with strike, maturity, and sentiment. Market stress can steepen that surface abruptly, and studies of cross-market volatility transmission show that uncertainty shocks can propagate across regions and asset classes rather than remain isolated [150].

Defined-risk structures: verticals, butterflies, condors, and collars

Defined-risk structures matter because they convert an open-ended opinion into a bounded economic contract. Instead of asking whether the underlying will move, the trader asks how much premium is worth spending or collecting to shape the payoff into a corridor, a ceiling, or a floor. That distinction is central in professional use. A defined-risk position does not eliminate uncertainty; it reallocates it into a form that can be budgeted, margined, and stress-tested with far more precision than an unhedged long or short option. The tradeoff is that the premium profile becomes more engineered, and the edge depends on whether the chosen boundaries match the actual market path.

Vertical spreads are the simplest expression of that logic. A bull call spread, for example, combines a long call with a higher-strike short call, while a bear put spread uses a long put with a lower-strike short put. In each case, one leg finances part of the other, reducing net premium outlay and capping both profit and loss. The structure is useful when the trader has a directional view but does not expect an outsized move beyond a certain level. It is also a cleaner way to express conviction when implied volatility is expensive, because the short leg partially offsets the volatility premium embedded in the long leg. The cost of that efficiency is obvious: the spread gives up unlimited upside in exchange for a more favorable entry price and a known maximum loss.

The practical appeal of verticals is that they reduce the problem from forecasting magnitude to forecasting a range. If the trader believes the underlying will move modestly in one direction, a spread can monetize that expectation without requiring a dramatic breakout. The short strike defines where additional movement stops adding value, so the position is less sensitive to tail outcomes than a naked option. That boundedness is not merely psychological; it changes the risk profile for capital allocation and position sizing. A desk can carry more notional spread exposure than naked option exposure because the worst-case outcome is pre-defined, although the aggregate risk still depends on correlation, liquidity, and the possibility of multiple spreads behaving badly at once.

Butterflies refine the same idea by targeting a narrow terminal zone. A standard butterfly combines two options at the wings and two at the body, creating a payoff that is highest near the middle strike and falls away on either side. This structure is often used when the trader expects the underlying to finish near a specific level or expects implied volatility to be overpriced relative to the realized move. The butterfly is attractive because its risk is limited and often relatively small compared with the potential reward if the market settles near the center strike. But that reward comes with a different burden: the structure is highly dependent on expiration behavior, and its value can erode quickly if the underlying drifts away from the target zone or if time decay works against the position before the expected pinning effect materializes.

Condors broaden the same concept by widening the profitable zone. A condor uses four strikes, typically producing a flatter payoff than a butterfly and a larger region of acceptable terminal prices. This makes condors useful when the trader expects limited movement but does not want to be overly precise about where the underlying will settle. The structure sacrifices peak payoff in exchange for a more forgiving range, which is often more realistic in markets that are range-bound but noisy. Credit condors, in particular, appeal to traders who want to collect premium while defining risk on both sides of the distribution. The position may look conservative because the loss is capped, but the trader is still short convexity across the range where the underlying can move enough to challenge one side of the structure without moving far enough to fully justify the premium collected.

The collar is different from the spread family because it is usually built around an existing asset position rather than a standalone directional view. A typical collar pairs a long put with a short call against a long stock or other underlying exposure. The put establishes downside protection, while the call finances part or all of that protection by surrendering some upside beyond the call strike. For institutions, collars are a practical compromise when the objective is not to maximize return but to preserve capital within a tolerable valuation band. They are common in equity portfolios, concentrated positions, and situations where a holder wants to reduce drawdown risk without fully liquidating the asset. The structure turns the underlying into a more bond-like instrument over the chosen horizon, though only within the boundaries set by the strike selection.

What unites these structures is that they are all forms of negotiated convexity. Each one decides where the trader wants to own optionality, where to sell it, and how much exposure to leave uncapped. That decision cannot be made in isolation from implied volatility, skew, and liquidity. A vertical that looks inexpensive may be poor value if the short strike is too close to a likely event move. A butterfly may appear attractive when the market is calm, only to become vulnerable if the underlying begins to trend. A condor may provide a wider profit zone, but the extra width can be costly if the wings are placed in thin markets. A collar may preserve capital, but it also creates an opportunity cost that becomes very visible in strong bull markets. Even the distribution of profits in these structures can be far from intuitive; empirical work on option trading has shown that payoff distributions are often non-normal, with distinct skewness and kurtosis characteristics depending on the structure [155].

For advanced practitioners, the important point is that defined-risk does not mean low-risk in any absolute sense. It means the loss profile is knowable in advance, which is valuable only if the trader is disciplined enough to respect the assumptions behind the trade. The strike spacing, expiration date, and premium balance all encode a view about price path, not just terminal price. If the market regime changes, the structure can shift from efficient to awkward very quickly. A defined-risk book therefore requires the same rigor as any other derivatives book: attention to margin, liquidity, assignment risk, and the possibility that a bounded loss on one position becomes an unbounded problem when multiplied across correlated exposures.

CHAPTER 6

Chapter 6: Advanced Structures and Institutional Strategy Design

Once the basic spread forms are understood, institutional design begins where standard templates stop being sufficient. At that level, the question is rarely whether a structure can be built, but whether it can be built to fit a mandate, a risk budget, a liquidity profile, and a governance process without introducing hidden convexity or unwanted path dependence. Large portfolios often need exposures that are more precise than a single option or a simple vertical can provide, yet still transparent enough to be monitored and defended under stress. The constructions that follow are therefore less about novelty than about control: shaping payoff geometry, aligning timing with funding and rebalancing constraints, and matching the instrument to the institution's operational reality.

Ratio spreads, diagonals, and complex spread construction

Ratio spreads, diagonals, and other complex spread structures are built from the same building blocks as verticals and calendars, but their purpose is different: they are designed to shape exposure more precisely than a simple one-for-one offset allows. In a ratio spread, the trader buys one option and sells a larger number of options at another strike, usually in the same expiration, creating a payoff that is intentionally unbalanced.

That imbalance can reduce or even eliminate the initial debit, but it also introduces a region where losses can expand if the underlying settles in the wrong area. The structure is therefore not a disguised bargain; it is a deliberate trade of premium efficiency for a more complicated risk profile. The trader is often seeking a specific directional zone, a favorable skew interaction, or a way to monetize an overpriced wing of the volatility surface without paying full price for the hedge.

The appeal of the ratio spread lies in its asymmetry. A call ratio spread, for example, may benefit from a moderate rise in the underlying while leaving the trader exposed if the market rallies too far beyond the short strike region. A put ratio spread can do the same on the downside, often with a view that price will move lower but not collapse. In both cases, the structure can produce a wide area of limited profit and a tail that requires active management. That tail is not an accidental flaw; it is the economic consequence of selling more optionality than is purchased. The position can be made less dangerous by selecting strikes farther apart, adding a protective long option, or converting the trade into a broken-wing structure, but each adjustment changes the distribution of outcomes and the margin requirement. The book value of the trade should never be confused with the risk budget it consumes.

Diagonals introduce a different dimension: time. A diagonal spread combines options with different expirations and, often, different strikes, so the trader is no longer just expressing a view on direction or terminal price but also on the term structure of volatility and the rate at which time value decays. A common diagonal might involve buying a longer-dated option and selling a shorter-dated option at a different strike. Compared with a pure calendar, the strike difference adds a directional bias; compared with a vertical, the differing expirations create a rolling time profile that can be harvested or managed over multiple cycles. This makes diagonals especially useful when the trader expects a slow move, a delayed catalyst, or a volatility term structure that is rich in the near term relative to the back month. The position can be adjusted as the short option decays, rolled forward, or re-centered to keep the exposure aligned with the evolving market.

What makes diagonals and ratios operationally important is that they are not just payoff diagrams; they are dynamic positions whose economics depend on path. A ratio spread may look attractive if the underlying finishes near the short strike, but its mark-to-market can deteriorate sharply if price accelerates through the danger zone before expiration. A diagonal may appear to be a low-cost way to hold exposure, yet its value can erode if the short leg decays more slowly than expected or if implied volatility shifts against the long leg. The trader is therefore managing not only delta, gamma, and theta, but also the interaction between strike selection, expiration mismatch, and the shape of the implied volatility surface. Because option surfaces are rarely flat, a spread that looks neutral in a pricing model can become directional in practice simply because the market prices different strikes and maturities differently. Studies of volatility smiles and surface dynamics have long emphasized that options are not redundant claims on a single state variable; they embed distinct exposures to the shape of the surface itself [161][86].

Complex spread construction becomes most useful when the objective is not to maximize payoff at a single point, but to define a probability-weighted region of acceptable outcomes. Traders combine ratios, diagonals, verticals, and sometimes additional legs to create structures that are flatter in the center, steeper at the edges, or more responsive to a particular expiration window. A position may be built to collect premium in a range, cap risk beyond that range, and preserve some convexity if the market moves faster than expected. The design process begins with the market view, but it cannot stop there. It must also account for liquidity, execution slippage, assignment risk, and the possibility that the position will need to be adjusted under stress rather than held to expiration. In institutional settings, this is where complexity becomes a governance issue as much as a trading issue: every additional leg adds another source of model error, correlation assumption, and operational failure.

The most disciplined way to construct these spreads is to start with the desired exposure map and work backward to the implementation. If the goal is to express a mildly bullish view with low upfront cost, a call ratio spread may be attractive only if the trader is willing to defend the upside tail. If the goal is to carry a long-dated directional view while financing it through short-term premium, a diagonal may fit better, provided the short leg can be rolled without excessive transaction costs. If the goal is to harvest skew or term-structure dislocations, the structure must be stress-tested across multiple price paths, not just at expiration. In practice, the same position can behave like a theta-positive income trade, a volatility trade, or a hidden directional bet depending on where the underlying trades and how the surface shifts. That is why complex spreads demand portfolio-level thinking. Their true risk is rarely visible in the initial premium alone; it emerges in the interaction between strikes, expirations, and the market's evolving distribution of uncertainty [162][85].

Volatility arbitrage, dispersion, and correlation trading concepts

Volatility arbitrage begins with the recognition that an option's market price and its realized payoff are not the same object. The trader is not simply betting on direction, but on the relationship between implied volatility, future realized volatility, and the cost of carrying a hedged book through time. In its most basic form, the trade is long or short volatility through options and dynamically offset in the underlying so that the residual P&L is driven more by the accuracy of the volatility view than by outright price direction. This is why the strategy is often discussed alongside delta hedging: the hedge is not a decorative risk reduction tool, but the mechanism that isolates the volatility exposure that the trader believes is mispriced.

That isolation is never perfect. Implied volatility embeds more than a forecast of future variance; it also reflects supply and demand for convexity, crash protection, balance-sheet constraints, and the market's willingness to pay for insurance. A desk that buys options because implied volatility looks cheap may still lose money if realized volatility is low but the hedge is expensive to maintain, if skew moves against the position, or if the underlying trends in a way that creates adverse re-hedging costs. Conversely, a seller of volatility can collect premium and still suffer if the market becomes disorderly, because the short-vol position is implicitly short convexity, short liquidity, and often short the ability to rebalance cheaply when the market gap widens. The lesson is that volatility arbitrage is a spread trade only in the broadest sense; the spread is between what the market is charging for uncertainty and what the trader expects to experience after hedging, financing, and transaction costs.

Dispersion trading takes that idea one level deeper by separating index volatility from single-name volatility. The index reflects not only the variance of its constituents, but also the correlation among them. That distinction creates a structural opportunity: if index implied volatility is rich relative to the implied volatilities of the components, a trader can buy or sell one side of the dispersion relationship by taking offsetting positions in the index and the basket of names. The classic institutional version is to be short correlation through an index option position while being long a basket of single-name options, or the reverse, depending on the relative pricing. The trade is not a pure volatility bet because the index's behavior depends on both constituent volatility and correlation. When correlations rise, the index can become more volatile even if individual names are not moving dramatically, and that can make a short-correlation position vulnerable precisely when diversification appears to be failing.

What makes dispersion attractive to sophisticated desks is that it allows the trader to express a view on the internal structure of the market rather than on the market's level. A portfolio manager may believe that company-specific event risk, earnings dispersion, sector rotation, or idiosyncratic shocks will dominate, keeping single-name volatility elevated relative to index volatility. In that case, long dispersion can monetize the gap between rich single-name option premiums and a cheaper index hedge. But the structure only works if the trader is disciplined about rebalancing weights, dividends, borrow costs, and the fact that the index and its components do not share identical contract terms or liquidity profiles. The strategy is therefore as much a relative-value and execution problem as it is a volatility view. The apparent elegance of the correlation trade can hide a large amount of operational friction.

Correlation trading is the most abstract of the three concepts, but in many ways it is the most important. Correlation is not directly traded in cash markets; it is inferred from the joint behavior of assets and embedded in option prices through the relationship between index variance and constituent variance. Because it is a derived quantity, it can move sharply when markets reprice systemic risk, even if the underlying assets themselves have not yet made extreme moves. In stressed periods, correlations often rise as investors de-risk together, and that is one reason index protection can become expensive relative to the volatility of the names inside the index. Historical crisis episodes showed how liquidity stress, forced deleveraging, and widening bid-ask spreads can overwhelm models that assume stable relationships among assets [1]. For a correlation trader, the issue is not merely whether correlations are "high" or "low," but whether they are stable enough to support hedging and whether the market is paying appropriately for the possibility that they will jump.

These trades also expose a recurring asymmetry in arbitrage: the price difference may be visible long before it becomes monetizable. Shorting rich index volatility against long single-name volatility, or the reverse, can look compelling on a screen while remaining fragile under financing stress, margin pressure, or sudden changes in liquidity. Research on hedge funds has shown that illiquidity can create serial dependence in returns and make apparent arbitrage profits difficult to realize smoothly [3]. That matters here because volatility and correlation trades often depend on frequent adjustments, and those adjustments are precisely what become expensive when the market is dislocated. A strategy can be statistically well founded and still be operationally weak if the path to convergence requires trading into widening markets or absorbing adverse mark-to-market moves before the pricing relationship normalizes.

For that reason, professional volatility, dispersion, and correlation books are managed as portfolios of risks, not as single opinions. The trader monitors the level of implied volatility, the slope of the term structure, the shape of skew, the concentration of event risk, and the stability of correlations across regimes. A book that is long single-name volatility and short index volatility may look neutral in aggregate, yet still carry hidden exposure to sector concentration, macro shocks, or liquidity cascades. The real craft is in making the position robust to the same forces that create the opportunity in the first place: changing correlations, unstable hedging costs, and market structure that can turn a relative-value edge into an absolute loss if the trade is too large, too levered, or too dependent on calm conditions.

Tail-risk hedging and crash protection frameworks

Tail-risk hedging is not a search for cheap protection; it is a deliberate attempt to own convexity when the portfolio's survival depends on it. The central problem is that crashes are not just larger versions of ordinary declines. They are regime changes in which correlations rise, liquidity weakens, and the instruments used to hedge can behave differently from the models that priced them. In practice, the hedge must be evaluated under conditions where the market is stressed enough that spreads widen, financing becomes more expensive, and the ability to rebalance is impaired. That is why a crash-protection framework has to be designed around what happens when the hedge is most needed, not around average behavior in calm markets.

The first design choice is the source of convexity. A long put is the most direct form of downside insurance, but the strike and tenor determine whether it is meaningful protection or merely symbolic coverage. Deep out-of-the-money puts can be inexpensive relative to the notional they reference, yet they often require a severe move before they contribute materially. Nearer-the-money puts cost more, but they begin to offset losses earlier and can reduce the gap between portfolio drawdown and hedge effectiveness. For institutions, the relevant question is not whether puts are "expensive," but whether the premium spent is small relative to the loss the portfolio is expected to absorb in a disorderly decline. That comparison must be made in the context of the book's actual beta, leverage, and liquidity profile.

A second choice is whether to own protection outright or finance it through premium harvesting elsewhere. Collars, put spreads, and overwrite programs are common because they convert some of the hedge cost into a trade-off against upside. That trade-off is not neutral. A collar may stabilize a portfolio's distribution, but it also caps part of the recovery that often follows sharp selloffs. Put spreads reduce premium outlay, yet they also limit the hedge precisely when the market falls far enough for insurance to matter most. The right structure depends on whether the mandate prioritizes drawdown containment, return preservation, or capital efficiency. In liability-driven or benchmark-sensitive mandates, the acceptable sacrifice of upside is often easier to justify than in absolute-return strategies that depend on participation in rebounds.

Crash protection also needs to be treated as a portfolio process rather than a single trade. A hedge that is effective at initiation may decay, become too far out-of-the-money, or lose relevance as the underlying portfolio changes. If the equity book becomes more concentrated, if credit spreads widen, or if volatility term structure steepens, the hedge ratio that once looked adequate may no longer cover the dominant risk. Dynamic maintenance matters, but so does restraint: overtrading a hedge can turn insurance into a separate speculative book. The framework should specify when protection is rolled, when it is resized, and when it is allowed to expire. Without that discipline, the hedge can become expensive in quiet markets and ineffective in violent ones.

For many institutions, the most robust crash-protection architecture combines several layers rather than relying on one instrument. A first layer may be structural de-risking through position limits or reduced gross exposure. A second layer may be index options that protect the broad market component of the portfolio. A third layer may be sector-specific or factor-specific hedges for books whose risk is more concentrated than the headline index suggests. This layered approach recognizes that a portfolio can be vulnerable to both market-wide drawdown and idiosyncratic clustering. It also acknowledges that not all losses arrive through the same channel; some emerge gradually through correlation creep, while others arrive abruptly through gap risk and liquidity failure.

The challenge is that crash hedges are often most valuable when market participants are already crowded into similar positions. In those moments, protection can become expensive exactly because everyone wants it at once. That crowding effect is one reason tail-risk programs must be considered over the full cycle rather than purchased only after volatility spikes. Historical episodes of financial stress show how quickly interconnected markets can transmit losses across institutions and asset classes [1][8][137][138]. For a hedge fund, insurer, or asset manager, the implication is straightforward: if the hedge is intended to defend against systemic stress, it should not assume that the rest of the market will remain orderly while the portfolio is under pressure.

There is also a difference between hedging price risk and hedging liquidity risk. A portfolio may appear protected on a mark-to-market basis and still fail operationally if the hedge cannot be monetized, rolled, or adjusted during the selloff. This is why practitioners often prefer instruments with deep secondary-market liquidity, transparent pricing, and well-understood margin behavior. In stressed markets, the ability to convert protection into cash or offset losses matters as much as the theoretical payoff. The hedge should therefore be evaluated not only by its terminal payout, but by its path dependence, financing demands, and sensitivity to market dislocations.

A disciplined crash-protection framework begins with a target loss threshold, then works backward to the payoff needed to keep the portfolio inside that boundary. That process forces clarity about what is being protected: a benchmark-relative drawdown, a capital base, a funding ratio, or a risk budget. Once the objective is explicit, the hedge can be sized to the exposure that threatens it, rather than to an abstract fear of market decline. Tail-risk hedging becomes most effective when it is integrated with governance, stress testing, and rebalancing rules, so that protection is not merely purchased, but continuously aligned with the portfolio it is meant to save.

Structured notes, overlays, and custom institutional implementations

Structured notes occupy a distinctive place in institutional derivatives practice because they are not simply trades; they are packaged solutions that combine funding, optionality, and distribution into a single instrument. The investor is not buying a naked option or a standalone swap but a note whose payoff is engineered around a reference asset, index, rate, basket, or commodity curve. That engineering can be useful when a mandate requires a specific risk profile that is difficult to source directly in the cash market. It can also obscure the economic transfer taking place if the structure is treated as a yield product rather than as a derivative with embedded contingencies. In professional settings, the first question is therefore not what coupon the note pays, but what risk the investor is being asked to warehouse in exchange for that coupon.

The design space is broad. A structured note may offer principal protection with limited upside participation, enhanced yield in exchange for selling volatility, or conditional exposure that depends on barriers, averages, or worst-of performance across several underlyings. Many notes are built from a bond component plus one or more embedded options, with the issuer using the option premium to finance the promised distribution. The investor receives a customized payoff, but customization comes at the cost of complexity in valuation, liquidity, and exit. Once the note is issued, the secondary market often reflects not only the embedded derivative value but also the issuer's credit spread, hedging costs, and any dealer margin embedded in the structure. For institutional buyers, that means the note must be evaluated as a package of market risk, credit risk, and documentation risk rather than as a single line item.

The most important analytical discipline is decomposition. A note that appears to offer attractive income may in fact be short volatility, short correlation, short tail protection, or short path independence. A coupon linked to equity performance can conceal a payoff that is favorable in calm markets but vulnerable to large gaps, volatility spikes, or repeated boundary tests. Autocallable structures, for example, can generate appealing carry by terminating early when markets rise, but they can also leave the investor exposed when markets drift lower and barriers remain unbreached. Range accruals, reverse convertibles, and step-up coupons each shift the balance between income and embedded risk in different ways, yet the same principle applies: the investor is being compensated for selling some combination of optionality, convexity, or adverse path dependence.

That same logic extends to overlays, which are usually better understood as portfolio-level risk transformation tools than as standalone instruments. An overlay does not replace the underlying portfolio; it sits on top of it to modify exposure, often with greater precision than a wholesale reallocation would allow. Equity index futures can adjust beta without liquidating securities. Options can reshape drawdown behavior without forcing a sale of long-term holdings. Swaps can alter duration, currency, or commodity exposure while preserving the core asset base. The appeal of overlays is operational as much as economic: they allow the manager to separate strategic holdings from tactical risk adjustments, which is particularly valuable when the underlying portfolio is constrained by taxes, mandates, illiquidity, or benchmark considerations [170][174][17].

In institutional implementation, the overlay is rarely a one-off trade. It is a governed process with explicit objectives, trigger levels, rebalancing rules, and attribution standards. A pension plan may use an overlay to reduce equity beta during periods of elevated risk without disturbing long-term strategic allocation. A sovereign or endowment portfolio may use a currency overlay to neutralize foreign-exchange noise while retaining foreign asset exposure. A commodity user may layer options on top of physical inventory or forward hedges to manage margin pressure and preserve budget stability. These programs work only when the institution distinguishes between the economic exposure it wants to keep and the risk it wants to outsource. Without that separation, overlays become ad hoc bets disguised as risk management.

Customization becomes most valuable when the institution's constraints are specific enough that off-the-shelf products are inefficient. Liability-driven investors may need exposures tied to discount rates, inflation, or long-dated cash flow matching. Insurance portfolios may require structures that manage capital charges as much as market volatility. Private wealth and family-office mandates often need solutions that reflect tax treatment, concentration risk, or spending requirements [17]. In these settings, a custom implementation may combine listed options, OTC swaps, and bespoke notes to fit a precise objective. The challenge is that every added layer of customization also adds model dependence, legal complexity, and counterparty exposure. A structure that is elegant in term-sheet form can become fragile if the hedging assumptions, settlement mechanics, or unwind provisions are not aligned with the portfolio's actual behavior.

For that reason, institutional governance matters as much as structuring skill. The desk designing the solution should be able to explain the embedded exposures in plain risk language: what happens if volatility rises, if correlation breaks down, if the underlying gaps through a barrier, or if liquidity disappears at the wrong time. Compliance and reporting systems increasingly have to support that transparency, and in many environments the control framework is becoming more automated because the complexity of the products exceeds what manual review can reliably police [99]. A custom implementation is only as strong as the institution's ability to monitor it after trade date. If the payoff cannot be decomposed, stress-tested, and attributed on an ongoing basis, then the structure may be too opaque for the mandate, regardless of how attractive the initial economics appear.

The practical standard is not whether a structured note or overlay is innovative, but whether it is economically legible. Institutional implementations should be built so that the investor can answer three questions at all times: what exposure is being earned, what exposure is being sold, and what conditions would cause the structure to fail to behave as intended. When those answers are clear, structured solutions can be powerful tools for tailoring risk in a way that cash instruments cannot. When they are not, the institution may be holding a more expensive and less liquid version of a risk it already knew how to own.

CHAPTER 7

Chapter 7: Derivatives in Portfolio Construction and Asset Allocation

Once derivatives move from isolated trades to portfolio tools, their role changes from expressing a view to shaping the structure of the entire risk budget. At that level, the question is not whether a contract is attractive on its own, but whether it improves the portfolio's balance between return, liquidity, and resilience under the constraints that govern real capital. This is where derivatives become a means of translation: converting cash exposure into something more efficient, more precise, or more defensible under stress. The same instrument can behave very differently depending on what it is being asked to replace, what risks it is meant to soften, and how it fits alongside the rest of the book.

Using derivatives to replace, enhance, or hedge cash positions

Derivatives can be used to alter a cash position without forcing the investor to sell the cash asset itself. That distinction matters because the economic objective is often not to abandon the underlying exposure, but to change its financing, risk, or payoff profile. A portfolio manager may want to keep a strategic equity holding, for example, while reducing short-term downside; a fixed-income desk may want to preserve a bond inventory while shortening duration; a commodity user may want to keep physical supply commitments intact while stabilizing price risk. In each case, the derivative becomes a layer on top of the cash position rather than a replacement for it, allowing the investor to separate ownership from exposure management.

Replacement is the most direct use case. A synthetic position can often reproduce the economic effect of holding an asset with less capital tied up in the cash market. A long stock position can be approximated with a long call and short put at the same strike and expiration, while a short stock exposure can be approximated with the opposite combination. Futures can also stand in for cash exposure when the objective is to maintain beta or commodity sensitivity without buying the physical asset. The appeal is not only efficiency but precision: the investor can decide whether the substitute should match the underlying one-for-one, only partially, or with a specific maturity profile. The tradeoff is that the replacement is never perfectly identical. Financing costs, dividend assumptions, roll costs, margin treatment, and the shape of the term structure all affect whether the synthetic truly behaves like the cash asset over the intended horizon.

Enhancement uses derivatives to modify a position that remains fundamentally intact. The cash asset stays in place, but the derivative adds a second layer of return or risk. A covered call on a stock portfolio is the classic example: the investor keeps the shares and sells call options to generate premium, effectively exchanging some upside for current income. A collar adds a put purchase to define the downside, financing that protection partly through call premium. In rates, an investor may hold a bond portfolio and use options or swaps to alter duration, convexity, or curve exposure without liquidating the bonds. Enhancement is attractive when the cash position carries strategic value that should not be disrupted, but the investor wants to shape the path of returns. The key is to recognize that enhancement is not free improvement; it is a deliberate transfer of one part of the payoff spectrum in exchange for another.

Hedging is the most familiar function, but in practice it is often more nuanced than simply "protecting against losses." A hedge may be designed to reduce delta, cap tail risk, offset a known liability, or stabilize reported performance over a specific accounting period. The hedge ratio becomes central because the objective is rarely to eliminate all risk. A partial hedge may be preferable if the investor wants to preserve some upside participation or avoid overpaying for protection. A pension fund might hedge part of its equity exposure with index futures while leaving some unhedged to maintain long-term growth potential. A commodity consumer may use options to protect against price spikes without giving up the benefit of lower prices. A bank may hedge a loan book or inventory with swaps or futures, not because the underlying assets are unwanted, but because the risk profile needs to be made more predictable.

The decision to replace, enhance, or hedge should begin with the cash position's economic role. Is the asset being held for return, liquidity, balance-sheet efficiency, regulatory treatment, or operational necessity? A position that is held for strategic reasons may be a poor candidate for outright sale, even if its risk profile needs adjustment. Derivatives are useful precisely because they let the investor preserve the economic function of the asset while changing the risk function. This is especially important when the cash market is illiquid, when transaction costs are high, or when selling the asset would trigger taxes, accounting consequences, or mandate violations. In those settings, the derivative is not a speculative overlay; it is a means of preserving the original portfolio architecture while improving its risk characteristics.

The practical challenge is that derivative overlays introduce basis risk. The cash asset and the derivative rarely move in perfect lockstep, and the mismatch can widen when volatility rises or liquidity deteriorates. Equity hedges may fail to track a concentrated portfolio if index composition differs materially from the holdings. Commodity hedges may underperform if the hedge instrument references a different grade, delivery point, or maturity than the physical exposure. Currency hedges can leave residual translation risk if the hedge horizon does not match the cash flow schedule. These mismatches are not defects in the instruments so much as reminders that the hedge is always an approximation. The more customized the cash exposure, the more carefully the derivative overlay must be calibrated.

For that reason, the best use of derivatives in this context is disciplined substitution, not mechanical substitution. The investor should ask what is being preserved, what is being transferred, and what is being paid for the transfer. If the goal is replacement, the derivative must be judged on how closely it reproduces the cash exposure under realistic financing and roll conditions. If the goal is enhancement, the added premium or carry must justify the surrender of part of the payoff. If the goal is hedging, the hedge must be evaluated under stress, not just under normal market conditions. In each case, derivatives are most effective when they are treated as tools for reshaping a cash position's economics rather than as a separate source of return detached from the underlying portfolio.

Portfolio insurance, drawdown control, and convexity management

Portfolio insurance is often discussed as if it were a single technique, but in practice it is a design problem: how to keep a portfolio within tolerable loss bounds without surrendering the return profile that justified the allocation in the first place. The economic objective is not to eliminate risk, which is impossible, but to make the portfolio's downside response more predictable across a range of market states. That can be done with listed puts, put spreads, collars, dynamic futures overlays, or combinations of these tools, but each method shifts the burden somewhere else. A put-based hedge converts part of the portfolio's ordinary market risk into an explicit premium cost. A dynamic hedge can reduce premium outlay, but it substitutes trading discipline and rebalancing risk. A collar may finance protection by capping upside, but it also changes the portfolio's participation in recoveries. The common thread is that insurance is never free; it is a transformation of risk, not its removal.

For institutional portfolios, the first question is usually not whether protection is desirable, but what kind of loss is being insured against. A manager with a long-only equity book may care about a broad drawdown caused by macro de-risking, while a liability-driven investor may be more concerned with a mismatch between asset values and liability discount rates. In the first case, index puts or futures-based overlays may be the most direct defense. In the second, the protection may need to be tied to rates, inflation, or cross-asset correlations rather than equity beta alone. This distinction matters because a hedge that is effective against one type of drawdown can be irrelevant against another. In asset-liability settings, the relevant question is often not the mark-to-market of the asset sleeve in isolation, but the change in surplus, funding ratio, or economic capital over the relevant horizon [35].

Drawdown control is therefore a policy choice as much as a trading choice. A portfolio can be managed to a maximum tolerated peak-to-trough decline by predefining triggers, hedge ratios, and rebalancing rules before stress arrives. Some allocators use static protection, accepting a recurring carry drag in exchange for simplicity and certainty. Others use conditional protection, adding hedges only when volatility, dispersion, or macro indicators indicate that the portfolio's loss distribution is becoming more skewed. Still others use systematic de-risking rules that reduce exposure as losses accumulate, though those rules can become procyclical if many market participants follow similar signals. The key is that drawdown control should be evaluated over an entire path, not just at expiration. A hedge that looks efficient at a single terminal date may be ineffective if the portfolio cannot survive the interim path to get there.

That path dependence is where convexity becomes central. Convexity is the feature that makes a portfolio's response to market moves nonlinear, and in risk management it is often the difference between a contained loss and a forced liquidation. Long options are the most obvious source of positive convexity, but convexity can also be created synthetically through rebalancing rules, spread structures, or overlays that become more protective as the market falls. The challenge is that positive convexity usually costs carry, while negative convexity often appears attractive because it generates income in calm markets. Investors who sell volatility, collect premium, or hold instruments with embedded short-option characteristics are effectively financing current returns by accepting a worse tail profile. That trade-off is manageable only if the portfolio's liquidity, leverage, and governance are robust enough to absorb the consequences when the convexity is called upon.

Convexity management is therefore not just about buying protection. It is about deciding where the portfolio should be long convexity, where it can afford to be short convexity, and how those exposures interact with the rest of the book. A pension fund, for example, may already have convexity embedded in its liability profile and may need assets that offset that asymmetry rather than add to it. A hedge fund may deliberately harvest short-volatility carry in one sleeve while maintaining explicit crash protection elsewhere. An energy or commodity book may use options to preserve upside participation while limiting the damage from a sudden collapse in prices. In each case, the portfolio designer is shaping the curvature of the payoff surface so that the book remains investable through stress, not merely profitable in benign conditions. The same logic appears in stochastic asset-liability optimization, where the objective is to balance expected growth against downside states that would impair the institution's ability to meet obligations [35].

The operational difficulty is that convexity is easiest to understand in theory and hardest to preserve in practice. A hedge that is intended to be protective can become a source of slippage if volatility spikes, liquidity thins, or the underlying gaps through the strike before the hedge can be adjusted. Dynamic insurance strategies, including futures-based rebalancing and volatility-targeting overlays, can reduce premium costs, but they depend on the assumption that markets remain tradable when the hedge must be changed. That assumption is weakest precisely when it matters most. For that reason, professional convexity management requires explicit attention to execution quality, margin usage, and the possibility that correlations break down under stress. The hedge should be tested not only for price sensitivity, but for the cost of implementation under adverse market conditions.

For sophisticated portfolios, the most effective insurance framework is usually layered. A core allocation may be left unhedged when the long-term expected return justifies the risk. A second layer may use modest, persistent protection to cap catastrophic loss. A third layer may be triggered only when risk indicators deteriorate or when the portfolio's own exposure map shows that convexity has become too negative. This layered approach avoids treating insurance as a binary decision. It recognizes that drawdown control is a budgeted function, just like transaction costs or financing. The aim is not to buy the most protection, but to buy the right amount of convexity at the right time, so that the portfolio can absorb shocks without being forced into behavior that destroys the original investment thesis.

Asset allocation overlays for equities, rates, commodities, and FX

Asset allocation overlays are most useful when they are treated as a second layer of portfolio design rather than as a trading add-on. The underlying cash portfolio remains the strategic anchor; the overlay modifies its factor exposure, hedges a discrete risk, or adjusts the timing of risk without forcing a wholesale sale of the assets themselves. That distinction matters because many institutional portfolios are built around mandates, benchmarks, tax constraints, liquidity needs, or liability structures that make direct reallocation expensive or operationally disruptive. An overlay allows the manager to preserve the core allocation while using derivatives to refine the portfolio's effective beta, duration, commodity sensitivity, or currency profile.

In equities, the most common overlay problem is not whether to own stocks, but how much market exposure to carry and under what drawdown profile. Index futures can increase or decrease beta quickly and with low transaction cost, which is why they are often used to keep a portfolio invested while cash is raised or reallocated elsewhere. Options add a different dimension by allowing the manager to define the downside in advance. A protective put overlay can convert an unbounded equity loss into a known premium cost, while a collar can finance part of that protection by giving up some upside. These are not interchangeable choices. Futures are efficient for linear exposure control; options are efficient when the objective is to reshape the return distribution itself. The right overlay depends on whether the portfolio needs temporary de-risking, persistent convexity, or a tighter tracking-error band around a benchmark.

Equity overlays also become more nuanced when the portfolio is not trying to eliminate risk but to separate broad market exposure from stock selection. A manager with strong alpha but unwanted beta can use index derivatives to isolate the active book, effectively expressing the view that the names held are attractive even if the market backdrop is not. This is one reason overlay programs are often discussed in the context of portable alpha and beta separation. In such structures, derivatives carry the market component while the cash portfolio is reserved for the idiosyncratic return source. The practical benefit is capital efficiency; the risk is that the hedge must be maintained with discipline, because beta is not static and the residual exposure can drift as correlations change. A portfolio that appears market-neutral in calm conditions may become directionally exposed when dispersion narrows or correlations rise.

In rates, the overlay problem is usually framed in duration, curve shape, and funding sensitivity rather than in simple directional terms. Futures on Treasury instruments, swaps, and swaptions can be used to lengthen or shorten portfolio duration without disturbing the underlying bond holdings. This is especially valuable for liability-driven investors, who care less about nominal bond price moves than about matching the present value of future obligations. The overlay may need to hedge not just level risk, but curve risk as well: a parallel shift in rates is only one of several ways a fixed-income portfolio can be stressed. A steepening or flattening move can change the value of assets and liabilities differently, so the derivative overlay has to be chosen with the shape of the curve in mind. When the objective is to preserve carry while controlling interest-rate exposure, the overlay often becomes a trade between precision and cost, because the cleanest hedge is not always the cheapest or most liquid one.

Commodity overlays are shaped by a different set of constraints. Here the issue is often not market beta but exposure to input costs, production margins, inventory values, or inflation-linked revenues. Producers and consumers rarely want to speculate on the outright level of the commodity; they want to stabilize the economics of the business. Futures can lock in a price, but they also remove upside participation. Options and option combinations are therefore useful when the business needs protection against adverse moves while retaining some benefit from favorable ones. A consumer exposed to rising energy costs may buy call options or structured call spreads to cap expense growth, while a producer may use puts or collars to protect revenue floors. The overlay must be aligned with the physical exposure, however, because commodity risk is often tied to basis, grade, location, and timing. A derivative that hedges the benchmark price imperfectly may still leave the operating business exposed to the spread that matters most.

FX overlays are especially important because currency risk is frequently a byproduct of investing rather than the primary source of return. International portfolios, cross-border operating businesses, and reserve managers all face the problem that asset performance can be overwhelmed by exchange-rate movement. The foreign exchange market is large, liquid, and structurally important because exchange rates influence output, inflation, capital flows, and the relative return on assets across countries [185]. That makes currency overlay a central tool in global portfolio construction. A manager may hedge foreign equity exposure back to the home currency to reduce volatility, leave part of the exposure unhedged to preserve diversification, or dynamically vary the hedge ratio depending on valuation, rate differentials, and risk appetite. For institutional investors, the decision is rarely binary. A partial hedge can reduce unwanted currency volatility while keeping some exposure to a foreign currency that may itself behave like a macro factor.

The mechanics of FX overlays also illustrate why derivative implementation matters as much as the strategic view. Forward contracts and currency swaps are often used because they are efficient for rolling hedges and matching settlement dates, while options are preferred when the investor wants asymmetric protection against a sharp currency move without giving up all favorable drift. In practice, the hedge ratio may be adjusted by currency pair, region, or asset class, because not all foreign exposures behave the same way. A portfolio holding foreign equities, foreign bonds, and overseas revenues may have multiple currency sensitivities that do not cancel neatly. Some institutions hedge only the developed-market currency basket and leave emerging-market currency exposure partly open because the cost of full hedging can be high and the underlying cash flows may already be volatile. Others use tactical overlays to respond to central bank policy divergence or balance-of-payments stress, but that requires a clear distinction between strategic currency policy and short-term market timing.

Across equities, rates, commodities, and FX, the common discipline is to define what the overlay is meant to change and what it is meant to leave untouched. A derivative overlay can reduce volatility, alter convexity, improve capital efficiency, or isolate a desired factor exposure, but it can also introduce roll cost, basis risk, liquidity dependence, and operational complexity. The portfolio manager therefore has to measure the overlay not only by its standalone P&L, but by how it changes the behavior of the whole book under stress, under carry, and through time. That is why overlays belong in the allocation process itself: they are part of the architecture of the portfolio, not merely a hedge placed on top of it.

Integrating derivatives into multi-asset and liability-driven portfolios

Integrating derivatives into a multi-asset portfolio is less about adding instruments than about deciding which risks should remain embedded in the cash book and which should be separated, resized, or transferred. A portfolio that spans equities, rates, commodities, and foreign exchange already contains a dense web of exposures: growth sensitivity, inflation sensitivity, duration, carry, funding stress, and currency translation. Derivatives give the manager a way to express those exposures explicitly instead of leaving them hidden inside the valuation of the underlying holdings. That explicitness matters because the same portfolio can look diversified in asset terms while remaining highly concentrated in macro factor terms. The practical task is to map the portfolio into its economic drivers and then decide where a derivative overlay improves the relationship between expected return, risk budget, and liquidity.

For multi-asset allocators, the first advantage of derivatives is precision. A cash portfolio is often too blunt to make small but meaningful adjustments without creating tax, trading, or mandate complications. Index futures can increase or reduce equity beta without disturbing the underlying stock selection. Treasury futures or swaps can alter duration without forcing bond sales across a ladder or benchmark sleeve. Commodity forwards can isolate price exposure from storage, transport, or operational considerations. FX forwards can neutralize currency translation so that a foreign asset allocation reflects the intended local risk rather than the investor's home-currency noise. In each case, the derivative is not replacing the investment thesis; it is refining the implementation so that the portfolio's measured risk aligns more closely with the intended one.

That refinement becomes more important when different asset classes interact. A portfolio that is long equities and long duration may be expressing a growth-sensitive profile that can become fragile in a regime shift. A commodity allocation may diversify inflation risk, but only if the exposure is not unintentionally amplified by currency movements or financing conditions. Cross-asset overlays let the manager separate these channels. The same institution can hold a strategic equity book, hedge part of the market beta with futures, use rate options to protect against abrupt yield moves, and use currency forwards to isolate the local return from the exchange-rate effect. The aim is not to make every sleeve market-neutral; it is to decide which correlations are acceptable and which are merely tolerated because the cash portfolio is not granular enough to eliminate them.

This logic extends naturally to liability-driven portfolios, where the benchmark is not an index but a stream of future obligations. Pension plans, insurers, endowments with spending rules, and asset managers with long-dated commitments all face the same structural problem: the assets are marked to market daily, while the liabilities are sensitive to discount rates, inflation, longevity, credit spreads, or policyholder behavior over long horizons. Derivatives allow the asset side to be shaped around the liability profile rather than around a generic return target. Interest rate swaps, bond futures, swaptions, and inflation-linked derivatives can be used to adjust duration, curve exposure, and convexity so that asset values move more consistently with the present value of obligations. Campbell's work on the yield curve underscores that short and long rates do not move in a mechanically simple way, which is precisely why liability hedging cannot rely on a single duration number alone [193].

A well-constructed liability-driven framework therefore distinguishes between funded status risk and return-seeking capital. The hedging portfolio is designed to absorb changes in discount rates, curve shape, and inflation assumptions with as little unintended basis risk as possible, while the return-seeking portfolio can remain focused on generating excess return. That separation is operationally useful because it prevents the institution from being forced to sell growth assets simply to manage balance-sheet volatility. In practice, the hedge may be implemented with a mixture of swaps, futures, and options depending on liquidity, collateral policy, and the need for convexity. A plain duration hedge may be adequate for a narrow liability profile, but many institutions need a more nuanced structure that accounts for nonparallel curve shifts, embedded guarantees, and the fact that liabilities themselves are often path dependent.

The more complex the liability, the more important it is to recognize that derivatives are not just hedging devices but tools for managing optionality already present in the institution's own balance sheet. Callable debt, pension guarantees, guaranteed minimum benefits, and inflation-linked spending rules all embed nonlinear exposure. Derivatives can either offset or replicate that optionality, but they must be chosen with an eye toward liquidity in stress conditions and the institution's ability to post margin. Systemic risk studies have shown how interconnected financial sectors can become, making it dangerous to assume that a hedge will remain isolated from broader market stress [137]. In a stressed environment, the same instruments used for protection may become more expensive to roll, more sensitive to basis changes, or more correlated with the liabilities they were meant to offset.

Implementation discipline is therefore as important as the overlay itself. A derivative overlay should be evaluated not only by its expected hedge effectiveness, but by its collateral demands, rebalancing frequency, accounting treatment, and governance burden. The manager must decide whether the portfolio is using derivatives to reduce risk, to transform it, or to defer it. Those are different objectives, and they can produce very different outcomes when markets gap, liquidity thins, or correlations break. In that sense, integrating derivatives into multi-asset and liability-driven portfolios is an exercise in balance-sheet engineering: using contracts to make exposures more legible, more portable, and more closely matched to the economic problem the portfolio is actually trying to solve.

CHAPTER 8

Chapter 8: Quantitative Modeling, Data, and Trading Systems

At this stage, the discussion shifts from what derivatives are and how they behave to how those behaviors are measured, tested, and operationalized inside a trading process. For experienced practitioners, the central issue is not whether a model can produce a price or a signal in isolation, but whether the surrounding data, assumptions, and system design can support decisions under real market conditions. Quantitative work in derivatives is especially sensitive to changing liquidity, shifting volatility, and the fact that market prices themselves often reflect stress, not just fundamentals; the 2007–2008 crisis made clear how quickly information can become fragmented when risk is embedded across linked instruments and balance sheets [1][10].

Building and validating quantitative trading models

Building a quantitative trading model for derivatives starts with a narrower question than many teams initially pose: what exact market inefficiency, pricing anomaly, or risk transfer are you trying to measure? A model that is supposed to forecast short-term option mispricing, estimate implied volatility dynamics, or rank relative value across strikes will fail if those objectives are blended together. The specification has to be explicit about the instrument universe, holding period, execution venue, and source of edge. In practice, the most durable models are not the most elaborate ones; they are the ones that define the trading problem cleanly enough that the signal can be tested against a realistic implementation path rather than an abstract return series.

That specification begins with data construction. Derivatives data are especially vulnerable to distortions because the recorded price is only one part of the economic state of the contract. Options require clean mappings between underlying, strike, expiration, exercise style, corporate actions, and contract adjustments. Futures and swaps require attention to roll conventions, delivery terms, funding assumptions, and any embedded seasonality. If the data are not normalized to a consistent contract schema, the model may appear to identify a pattern that is really just a change in contract composition or a stale quote. For that reason, the first validation step is not a forecast test but a data audit: quote quality, survivorship bias, missing observations, timestamp alignment, and the treatment of crossed or locked markets.

Feature design should follow the economics of the instrument rather than the convenience of the dataset. In derivatives, the most useful predictors often come from state variables that are already known to matter: moneyness, time to expiration, term structure, realized-versus-implied volatility spreads, skew, liquidity measures, and regime indicators. But the feature set must also be constrained by tradability. A variable may be statistically significant and still unusable if it depends on information that would not have been available at the decision time, or if it requires a hedge ratio that cannot be implemented without excessive turnover. This is where many otherwise sophisticated models fail: they describe price behavior well in sample but ignore the friction of turning that description into a position.

Model choice should match the structure of the problem. Linear models remain useful when the objective is interpretability, fast recalibration, or stable factor attribution. Tree-based methods and other nonlinear approaches can capture interactions among volatility, liquidity, and macro conditions that a linear specification may miss. Sequence models may be appropriate when the signal depends on path dependence, order flow, or evolving term structure. Yet greater flexibility increases the burden of validation. The more expressive the model, the easier it is to fit noise, especially in derivatives markets where the number of genuinely independent observations can be much smaller than the raw row count suggests. Machine learning has become an important tool in financial risk management, but the literature also emphasizes that the gain depends heavily on disciplined feature control, validation design, and problem framing [109].

Validation should be built around the way the strategy will actually be traded. Random train-test splits are usually inappropriate for time-dependent derivatives data because they leak future regime information into the past. Walk-forward testing, rolling recalibration windows, and out-of-sample evaluation by market regime are more informative. If the model is intended for option selection, the test should include the full chain of candidate contracts, not just a single benchmark strike. If the model is intended for hedging, the evaluation should measure hedge error, turnover, and tail behavior, not only forecast accuracy. A model that slightly improves mean prediction but doubles rebalancing cost or worsens crash performance is not better in a trading sense.

Robustness checks matter because derivatives strategies are often built on thin statistical margins. Small changes in transaction costs, implied volatility inputs, or execution timing can erase an apparent edge. Sensitivity analysis should therefore vary not only model parameters but also the assumptions surrounding them: bid-ask width, slippage, delay, margin usage, contract liquidity, and roll timing. Stress tests should include volatility shocks, correlation breakdowns, and jumps in the underlying, because these are the conditions under which option books and hedges are most likely to behave differently from the backtest. Quantitative work in finance increasingly borrows methods from stochastic programming and scenario-based optimization because point estimates alone are not enough when the portfolio must remain viable across uncertain states [35].

Overfitting is especially dangerous in derivatives because the space of possible explanations is so large. A model can appear to work by exploiting a narrow expiration window, a single volatility regime, or a historical quirk in contract selection. The usual defenses apply—penalization, feature reduction, and out-of-sample testing—but derivatives modeling also benefits from economic restrictions. A signal should be rejected if it implies implausible trading frequency, inconsistent exposure to known risk factors, or dependence on information that would be impossible to monetize at scale. Research on hedge fund holdings has shown that observable portfolio construction often hides a great deal of the true strategy, which is a reminder that apparent complexity can conceal fragile or crowded exposures rather than durable skill [195].

Finally, model validation is not complete until the output is embedded in a governance process. The model should produce not only a trade signal but also an explanation of confidence, exposure, and failure conditions. That means documenting the data lineage, versioning the code, monitoring drift, and defining when the model should be suspended or recalibrated. For derivatives desks, this is not a bureaucratic layer added after the fact; it is part of the model itself, because the value of any forecast depends on whether the system can still trust it after the market changes. As capital regulation and funding conditions can alter risk-taking incentives and market behavior, the model's assumptions should be revisited whenever the surrounding balance-sheet environment changes materially [6].

Volatility modeling, implied surfaces, and scenario analysis

Volatility modeling is the bridge between a quoted option premium and the trader's actual belief about how uncertain the underlying path is likely to be. A single volatility input is often sufficient for a textbook pricing exercise, but it is rarely enough for a live book. In practice, realized volatility is not constant, implied volatility is not flat across strikes or expirations, and the relationship between the two changes as market regimes shift. For that reason, desks model volatility as a state variable with memory, clustering, and mean-reverting tendencies rather than as a fixed assumption. The objective is not to predict the future exactly, but to describe it in a way that is stable enough to support pricing, hedging, and capital allocation.

At the most basic level, volatility models attempt to separate the persistent features of the market from the noise. Historical estimates remain useful as a starting point, but they are backward-looking and can be badly misaligned with the risk embedded in current option prices. More sophisticated approaches incorporate conditional variance, jumps, and regime changes so that the model can react when the market shifts from calm to stressed behavior. This matters because an option book is exposed not only to the level of volatility, but to the path by which that volatility arrives. A slow drift higher in realized variance can have a very different effect from a sudden repricing triggered by an event or liquidity shock.

The implied volatility surface is where these ideas become visible in market terms. Rather than assigning one volatility number to an entire expiration, the surface maps implied volatility across strikes and maturities. Its shape usually reflects three persistent features: a term structure that can rise or fall across expirations, a skew or smile that shows how the market prices out-of-the-money versus near-the-money options, and local distortions around events or supply-demand imbalances. For equity options, the downside skew often reflects the market's willingness to pay for crash protection, while in other asset classes the structure may look different depending on carry, seasonality, or convexity demand. A surface is therefore not just a mathematical object; it is a record of how participants are distributing risk across states of the world.

For advanced practitioners, the key issue is that the surface is dynamic and internally connected. A change in one strike or maturity rarely occurs in isolation. If the front end of the curve reprices after a macro release, the entire surface may shift, but not uniformly. If demand concentrates in a narrow part of the chain, the resulting dislocation can create relative-value opportunities as well as hedging problems. Calibration then becomes a practical exercise in balancing smoothness against fidelity. A surface that is too rigid will miss real market structure; one that is too flexible can fit noise and produce unstable hedge ratios. This tension is a classic form of model risk, and its importance in derivatives valuation has been emphasized in the literature [198].

Scenario analysis is the discipline that keeps volatility modeling from becoming an exercise in curve fitting. A model may produce a coherent surface today, but a portfolio must still be evaluated under alternative states: a volatility spike with unchanged direction, a sharp equity selloff with widening skew, a rate shock that changes discounting and implied vol together, or a quiet market in which realized volatility collapses while implied premiums remain elevated. Scenario analysis should therefore move beyond simple up-and-down price shocks and explicitly vary volatility level, skew slope, term structure, correlation, and liquidity assumptions. The point is to test how the position behaves when the surface itself moves, not merely when the underlying moves along a fixed surface.

This is especially important because option P&L often comes from interactions among variables rather than from any single input. A long convexity position may look attractive if only spot is shocked, but its performance can deteriorate if implied volatility falls faster than the underlying moves. A short-volatility portfolio may appear tolerable under small daily shocks yet fail badly when a volatility regime shift expands both tails of the distribution and the bid-offer spread at the same time. Scenario analysis should therefore be linked to hedging logic: what gets rebalanced, what gets left exposed, and what liquidity is assumed to exist when the portfolio is under stress. In that sense, the scenario is not a forecast but a controlled failure test.

There is also value in comparing model-implied scenarios with market-implied ones. If the surface suggests that the market is pricing persistent downside protection, but the desk's own model expects volatility to mean-revert quickly, the gap is not merely theoretical. It can affect relative-value trades, hedge timing, and the interpretation of carry. Research has shown that implied volatility surfaces contain economically meaningful information about volatility risk and pricing kernels, not just statistical noise [147][86]. For a practitioner, that means the surface should be read as a live negotiation between supply, demand, and forward uncertainty. The best use of scenario analysis is to identify where the desk's assumptions differ from that negotiation and to decide whether the discrepancy is a source of edge or a source of hidden risk.

Backtesting pitfalls, overfitting, and robustness checks

Backtests are useful because they force a strategy to confront history, but history is not a neutral laboratory. A derivative strategy is shaped by execution frictions, margin rules, volatility regimes, corporate actions, contract specifications, and the path dependence created by rolling and rebalancing. A clean equity-style backtest that simply applies end-of-day signals to a closing price series often misses the very features that make options and other derivatives behave differently from linear assets. The result can be a performance curve that looks precise while quietly omitting the costs, timing effects, and discontinuities that would dominate live trading.

The most common pitfall is to confuse a model that explains the past with one that can survive the future. Overfitting appears when a strategy is tuned so aggressively to the historical sample that it begins to capture noise, temporary market structure, or a handful of favorable episodes rather than a stable economic relationship. This problem is especially acute in derivatives because the number of available degrees of freedom is large: strike selection, expiration choice, roll timing, delta targeting, volatility filters, entry thresholds, and exit rules can all be adjusted until the backtest fits almost any preferred narrative. Research on factor-based investing has shown how easy it is for investors to get lost in a large universe of candidate signals, and the same logic applies to option strategies: the more parameters a process exposes, the more care is needed to separate genuine structure from accidental fit [202].

In practice, overfitting often hides behind performance metrics that reward smoothness too much. A strategy with a high Sharpe ratio, limited drawdowns, and a visually attractive equity curve may still be fragile if those results depend on a narrow range of dates, a single volatility regime, or an execution assumption that is unrealistically favorable. One warning sign is instability: if small changes in lookback window, strike distance, or rehedging frequency produce large swings in results, the apparent edge may be mostly a product of parameter luck. Another warning sign is excessive complexity relative to the economic hypothesis. If a strategy requires many filters to work, it may be explaining the sample rather than exploiting a tradable inefficiency.

Robustness checks are the practical defense against this failure mode. The first test is usually out-of-sample validation, but that should not be treated as a box to check once. A more reliable process uses multiple layers: a training period, a validation period for design choices, and a genuinely untouched test period for final evaluation. Walk-forward analysis is often more informative than a single static split because it repeatedly re-estimates the model using only information that would have been available at the time. For options strategies, this matters because implied volatility, skew, and term structure are regime-sensitive; a model calibrated in one market environment may behave very differently in another.

Stress testing should be broader than simply shocking the underlying price. A derivative backtest should also perturb implied volatility, bid-ask spreads, borrow costs, funding rates, dividend assumptions, and the timing of rolls or expirations. For short-volatility or premium-selling strategies, the critical question is not whether the strategy earned carry in normal periods, but how it behaves when volatility jumps, correlations rise, and liquidity deteriorates simultaneously. Synthetic-data approaches and simulation methods can help explore rare states that are underrepresented in the historical record, although they must be used carefully because the simulation itself can import assumptions that are just as restrictive as the original model [203].

Another essential check is sensitivity analysis. A robust strategy should not depend on a single perfect input estimate. If a small change in the volatility forecast, transaction cost estimate, or fill assumption destroys the economics, the strategy is probably too brittle for institutional use. This is especially important when the backtest uses midquotes or assumes immediate execution at theoretical prices. Real option trading occurs across a spread, often with size constraints and limited depth, so a backtest that ignores slippage can convert a marginal strategy into a seemingly exceptional one. The more frequently a strategy trades or rebalances, the more that omission matters.

There is also a structural bias in financial backtesting that is easy to overlook: the data-generating process itself changes. Contract listings expand, market makers adapt, volatility targeting becomes crowded, and regulatory or margin changes alter the economics of holding risk. Historical option data can therefore be informative without being stationary. A strategy that worked because it exploited a particular market microstructure may stop working once the opportunity becomes widely observed. That is why robustness should include regime segmentation, subperiod analysis, and a check for whether the edge survives across different volatility environments, rate regimes, and liquidity conditions. Studies of hedge-fund behavior and dynamic strategies emphasize that performance often depends on exposures that evolve over time rather than on a single static alpha source [175].

For advanced practitioners, the goal is not to eliminate backtesting; it is to make it honest enough to support capital allocation. A credible research process asks whether the result persists after reasonable changes to assumptions, whether the economic rationale is clear enough to survive different samples, and whether the live implementation can reproduce the tested behavior after costs. When a strategy only works under the most favorable interpretation of the data, it is not robust. When it continues to work after the model is simplified, the sample is perturbed, and the execution assumptions are tightened, the backtest begins to resemble something closer to a tradable proposition than a historical coincidence.

Execution, slippage, transaction costs, and automation considerations

Execution quality often determines whether a theoretically sound derivatives strategy survives contact with the market. A model may identify the right direction, the right strike, and the right expiration, yet still fail because the order entered the market at the wrong time, crossed too much spread, or interacted poorly with a thin book. In derivatives, the gap between indicated price and executable price can widen quickly because quoted markets are shaped by inventory, hedging pressure, and the urgency of other participants. That is why execution should be treated as part of the strategy itself rather than as a mechanical afterthought. The economic value of an edge is not the paper alpha generated by a signal; it is the alpha remaining after the trade is actually established, adjusted, rolled, and unwound.

Slippage is the first visible cost of imperfect execution, but it is not a single phenomenon. It includes the bid-ask spread paid on entry and exit, the market impact created by order size relative to available liquidity, and the adverse movement that occurs while an order is working. In options, these effects can be amplified by contract granularity and by the fact that liquidity is often concentrated in a narrow set of strikes and expirations. A strategy that appears efficient on mid-market marks may be much less attractive once the trader repeatedly pays half-spreads across multiple legs. For multi-leg structures, the cost is not merely additive; one leg may fill while another does not, leaving the book temporarily exposed to directional or volatility risk. That partial-fill risk is especially important in fast markets, where the underlying can move enough between legs to alter the expected profile of the entire package.

Transaction costs should therefore be modeled as a distribution, not a constant. The visible commission or exchange fee is usually the smallest component. More consequential are spread costs, financing costs, exercise and assignment frictions, margin usage, and the hidden cost of capital tied up while a position is held. For institutional desks, the relevant question is often not whether a strategy has positive expected gross return, but whether that return survives the cumulative drag of rolling, rebalancing, and hedging. This is particularly true for strategies that trade frequently or that require dynamic adjustment as delta, gamma, or volatility exposure changes. A high-turnover book can look robust in a backtest and still underperform because the realized implementation cost is consistently higher than assumed. In energy and commodity markets, where shocks can be abrupt and liquidity can thin around events, the cost of reaching or exiting a hedge can become a material part of the trade's economics [215].

Execution design should match the purpose of the trade. If the objective is to acquire a position with minimal leakage, patience and price discipline may matter more than immediacy. If the objective is to neutralize risk quickly, speed may justify paying more. That trade-off becomes most visible in options spreads and volatility structures, where the difference between an all-or-none package fill and a piecemeal execution can change the risk profile materially. Order type selection matters because market orders maximize certainty of fill while limiting control over price, whereas limit orders protect price but increase the chance of missed execution or stale exposure. For larger books, slicing orders, staging entries, and using execution windows tied to liquidity conditions can reduce impact, but only if the trader understands the market's microstructure and the contract's actual depth rather than relying on displayed quotes alone.

Automation changes the implementation problem without eliminating it. Algorithmic execution can improve consistency, reduce latency, and enforce discipline in order placement, re-hedging, and roll management. It can also create new failure modes when models are too rigid, data feeds are delayed or corrupted, or routing logic reacts to transient noise as if it were a durable signal. Automated systems are particularly sensitive in derivatives because small input errors can propagate into large risk changes when leverage and convexity are involved. Research on automated trading has emphasized that algorithmic systems can generate disruptive behavior if they are not properly constrained and monitored [213]. In practice, that means automation should be paired with explicit guardrails: position limits, kill switches, fill-quality checks, stale-quote filters, and escalation rules for abnormal market conditions. Real-time data integration is increasingly important because delayed inputs can produce decisions that are optimal only in a static world, not in the live environment where spreads, volatility, and hedge ratios are continuously changing [212].

The best automation frameworks preserve human judgment at the points where model assumptions are most fragile. A system can decide how to work an order, but a trader or risk manager should define when the system is allowed to trade, what conditions invalidate the signal, and how exceptions are handled. This is especially relevant when the strategy depends on implied volatility surfaces, cross-asset hedges, or correlations that can shift abruptly. Automation can also help standardize post-trade analysis by comparing expected versus realized fill quality, tracking implementation shortfall, and identifying whether losses came from signal error or execution error. That distinction matters because a strategy that is marginal before costs may still be useful if execution can be improved, while a strategy that is profitable before costs may be untradeable if it requires persistent liquidity that the market does not reliably provide.

For institutional users, the operational question is not whether automation should be used, but where it belongs in the workflow. Routine hedges, systematic rolls, and repetitive rebalancing tasks are natural candidates because they benefit from speed and consistency. Discretionary overlays, event-sensitive trades, and positions with fragile liquidity often require tighter human supervision. The broader point is that execution quality, cost control, and automation architecture all shape the realized payoff distribution of a derivatives program. A strategy that ignores them is not simply incomplete; it is mismeasured.

CHAPTER 9

Chapter 9: Risk Management, Stress Testing, and Failure Prevention

Risk management in derivatives is not a separate administrative layer added after a trade is placed; it is the framework that determines whether the trade can be held through ordinary volatility, funding pressure, and the occasional break in market assumptions. Because derivatives can concentrate exposure so efficiently, the first failure mode is often not the strategy itself but the gap between intended risk and realized risk once position size, financing, and liquidity interact. That is why the discussion that follows moves from sizing and leverage restraint to scenario design, then to the operational realities of counterparty exposure, margin, and collateral, and finally to the controls that keep a book governed rather than merely monitored.

Position sizing, leverage limits, and capital preservation rules

Position sizing in derivatives should be defined in economic terms before it is ever expressed in contracts. The relevant question is not how many option contracts can be bought or sold, but how much of the portfolio's capital, margin capacity, and risk budget is being committed to a given exposure if the trade moves against the book, gaps through the hedge, or becomes temporarily illiquid. For linear instruments, notional value can sometimes serve as a rough proxy for exposure; for options, that shortcut is often misleading because premium, delta, gamma, and the path of the underlying all matter simultaneously. A position that looks small on premium outlay can still carry large directional, volatility, or tail exposure once the contract is stressed across plausible scenarios.

The practical unit of sizing is therefore the loss the portfolio can absorb under adverse but credible conditions. That means sizing should be tied to a precommitted risk measure, not to conviction alone. For a long option, the premium is the maximum loss, but the trade can still be oversized if the cumulative premium spend becomes large relative to the portfolio's return stream or if the strategy relies on repeated premium purchases that create a slow bleed. For a short option, the initial credit can obscure how quickly the position can expand into a large loss when volatility rises or the underlying moves sharply. In both cases, the correct sizing discipline begins with defining how much of the portfolio may be exposed to one scenario, one underlying, one event window, or one correlated cluster of positions.

Leverage limits are the mechanism that keeps that sizing discipline from being overridden by the apparent efficiency of derivatives. Because derivatives convert a modest cash commitment into a larger economic exposure, leverage should be measured at several levels at once: gross notional, net directional exposure, margin usage, and stress loss under shocks. A book can appear modest on a mark-to-market basis while still being highly levered if it depends on stable financing, low volatility, or continuous access to liquidity. This is one reason quantitative portfolio restrictions have long been used in institutional settings, especially where the objective is to avoid concentration and forced liquidation rather than to maximize short-term return [226].

For advanced practitioners, leverage limits are most effective when they are not a single hard ceiling but a layered set of guardrails. A desk may cap gross notional relative to capital, cap delta-equivalent exposure relative to equity, and separately cap vega, gamma, or concentrated event risk. It may also impose tighter limits when implied volatility is low, when liquidity is thin, or when the position is in a name with correlated exposures elsewhere in the book. This matters because leverage is not static; it changes as markets move. A short-dated option that was comfortably sized in the morning can become materially larger by the afternoon if gamma accelerates the delta profile or if the underlying moves toward a strike where exposure becomes more nonlinear.

Capital preservation rules are the backstop that prevents a strategy from surviving in theory but failing in practice. The first rule is that no single trade should be allowed to threaten the continuity of the portfolio. The second is that a sequence of losses must be survivable without forcing liquidation of unrelated positions at unfavorable prices. The third is that capital committed to derivatives should remain available for margin, variation margin, and opportunistic rebalancing during stress. These rules are especially important in markets where loss information can become difficult to interpret precisely when interlinked positions are under pressure, a dynamic that was central to the 2007 crisis [10]. In such periods, the danger is not only the size of the loss but the speed with which uncertainty about that loss can spread through the system.

Capital preservation also requires distinguishing between a tolerable drawdown and a regime change. A portfolio can absorb ordinary losses, but once losses begin to alter financing terms, collateral availability, or investor confidence, the problem is no longer just volatility but structural fragility. This is why ex ante limits matter even in markets that can be managed ex post through liquidation or legal remedies; financial systems are interdependent, and once stress begins, the cost of failure can propagate beyond the original position [223]. For that reason, many institutional mandates rely on predefined stop levels, exposure reduction triggers, and escalation procedures rather than discretionary judgment alone. The goal is not to remove discretion, but to ensure that discretion operates inside a framework that assumes adverse conditions will eventually arrive.

In practice, a robust sizing framework combines portfolio-level and trade-level controls. At the trade level, the position should be justified by its expected contribution to return, hedge efficiency, or convexity, and then translated into a maximum acceptable loss under multiple shocks. At the portfolio level, the combined effect of all positions should be monitored for concentration, correlation, and liquidity overlap. A portfolio can have several individually acceptable trades that become unacceptable when they share the same hidden risk factor, such as volatility expansion, funding stress, or a common macro catalyst. That is why capital preservation cannot be reduced to stop-loss rules alone; it requires an ongoing comparison between intended exposure and realized sensitivity, with the discipline to reduce size when the relationship drifts.

The most reliable rule is simple: size the position so that the portfolio can be wrong, early, and temporarily illiquid without losing the ability to continue. That standard is more demanding than a volatility target or a margin test, but it is the standard that keeps derivatives from turning a controlled risk transfer into a forced exit. In a professional setting, the objective is not merely to avoid a single catastrophic loss, but to preserve the optionality of the capital itself so that the book remains able to adapt when the market changes character.

Stress testing, scenario analysis, and tail-event planning

Stress testing begins where standard risk metrics stop being comfortable. A portfolio that looks balanced under small, independent moves can behave very differently when prices gap, correlations converge, liquidity thins, and financing becomes scarce at the same time. The point is not to predict the exact crisis that will occur; it is to force the book through states of the world in which the assumptions behind daily risk reports are least reliable. Value at risk is useful as a baseline because it formalizes exposure under ordinary conditions, but even the classic introduction to VaR treats it as one tool among several, not a complete answer to tail risk [91]. For derivatives, the weakness is especially clear: the same position that appears manageable under a variance-covariance model may produce nonlinear losses once volatility jumps, skew steepens, or hedges become expensive to maintain.

The first design choice in a stress program is whether to use historical, hypothetical, or blended scenarios. Historical shocks anchor the analysis in episodes that actually occurred, which helps prevent complacency and forces the portfolio to confront the kinds of discontinuities that often appear in real crises. Hypothetical scenarios are equally important because the next disruption rarely matches the last one exactly. A rate shock, an equity drawdown, a commodity supply interruption, or a currency devaluation may combine in a way that has no perfect historical analogue. In practice, the most useful framework is a layered one: start with known crisis patterns, then overlay targeted shocks to the variables that matter most to the book, including spot price, implied volatility, term structure, correlation, funding spread, and bid-ask width. That combination is more informative than any single number because it shows not only how much the portfolio can lose, but how those losses are distributed across time and market state.

For options and other convex instruments, scenario analysis should be built around the actual path of the underlying rather than a single endpoint. A short option position can look harmless if one only asks where the market finishes at expiration, yet the same position may become unmanageable if the underlying first moves violently against the book, forcing margin calls or hedging at unfavorable prices. Conversely, a long convex structure may appear expensive under a static mark, but it can become valuable precisely because it gains when the market is least liquid and most dislocated. This is why advanced stress tests should include path-dependent sequences such as a sharp gap followed by partial recovery, a slow grind lower with volatility compression, or a fast rally that crushes short-volatility carry before the hedge can be adjusted. These paths matter because derivative P&L is often realized through the interaction of Greeks over time, not just through the final settlement level.

Tail-event planning goes beyond measuring the loss to deciding in advance what the portfolio will do when the loss is already unfolding. That means identifying trigger points for reducing exposure, rolling hedges, raising collateral, or suspending strategies whose edge depends on stable liquidity. In a stressed market, the most damaging mistake is frequently not the original position but the refusal to change the plan when the regime has clearly changed. The book should therefore be organized around precommitted actions: which trades can be cut immediately, which can be financed through temporary volatility, which require counterparty communication, and which must be left alone because forced liquidation would do more harm than patience. The design objective is to avoid improvisation at the worst possible time, when spreads have widened and execution quality has deteriorated.

Liquidity deserves special treatment in tail planning because it is both a market variable and a risk multiplier. During periods of stress, the ability to exit or rebalance can deteriorate faster than the underlying price itself. That is not merely an inconvenience; it changes the economic meaning of the position. A hedge that is theoretically effective but practically untradeable can fail exactly when needed most. The crisis literature repeatedly shows that market stress and liquidity stress tend to reinforce each other rather than offset each other [1][98][55]. For derivatives desks, that means stress tests should not assume the hedge can be implemented at the last observed quote. Instead, they should model slippage, wider spreads, reduced depth, and the possibility that correlated instruments all become expensive to transact at once. In severe episodes, even assets normally treated as safe or liquid can experience temporary dislocation [231], which makes contingency planning more than a theoretical exercise.

Tail-event planning also has to account for the funding side of the book. Derivatives can create exposure that is small in premium terms but large in margin terms, and the margin requirement itself can rise just as the portfolio is losing value. A stress framework should therefore test the interaction between mark-to-market losses, collateral calls, and the availability of cash or financing. That is particularly important for portfolios that rely on short premium, relative value, or dynamic hedging, because the strategy may remain economically sound while still becoming operationally fragile. A well-designed plan distinguishes between risk of loss and risk of forced liquidation. The first is a market problem; the second is a survivability problem. In practice, the second often determines whether the first becomes permanent.

At an institutional level, the most effective stress process is one that is repeated, documented, and tied to decision rights. Scenarios should be updated as the portfolio changes, not treated as an annual compliance ritual. The results should be reviewed not only by traders but by risk managers, treasury, and senior decision-makers who control capital and limits. When a scenario shows that a position is vulnerable to a 20 percent gap, a volatility doubling, or a liquidity freeze, the relevant question is not whether the scenario is likely; it is whether the organization has already agreed on the response. That discipline is what turns stress testing from a reporting exercise into a usable defense against tail dependence, because the goal is not to eliminate extreme outcomes but to ensure that extreme outcomes do not also become existential ones.

Counterparty risk, margining, and collateral management

Counterparty risk is the possibility that the other side of the contract fails to perform when performance matters most. In derivatives, that failure is not a peripheral inconvenience; it can change the economics of the trade itself. A position that appears fully hedged in mark-to-market terms may still leave the holder exposed if the counterparty cannot pay variation margin, return collateral, or settle the final obligation. This is why credit analysis and trade structuring cannot be separated. The same contract can be nearly riskless when cleared through a well-capitalized central counterparty and materially more fragile when documented bilaterally with a thinly capitalized dealer, a concentrated hedge fund, or a special purpose vehicle whose liabilities depend on funding continuity. The 2007–2008 crisis showed how quickly uncertainty about where losses reside can propagate through interlinked securities and derivatives [10].

In practice, counterparty exposure is not static. It changes with market moves, netting arrangements, the quality and haircut of posted collateral, and the legal enforceability of the master agreement. A swap or OTC option may be economically small at inception and become highly exposed after a sharp move in the underlying, because the in-the-money side accumulates a receivable that must be collected later. That receivable is only as good as the counterparty's ability to pay and the documentation that governs closeout. Netting helps by compressing positive and negative exposures into a single obligation set, but netting is most effective when the same legal entity, the same agreement, and the same collateral terms apply across the book. Fragmented documentation or weak collateral terms can leave the trader with several small-looking trades that add up to one large credit problem.

Margining is the mechanism that converts market risk into funding discipline. In cleared markets, initial margin is posted up front to cover potential future exposure over a liquidation horizon, while variation margin transfers daily gains and losses as the position moves. That daily settlement process is one of the main reasons listed derivatives are structurally more robust than many bilateral contracts: losses are not allowed to accumulate indefinitely inside the system. But margining is not a neutral administrative detail. It creates liquidity demands that can be just as dangerous as the original market exposure. A position can be fundamentally sound and still become unmanageable if adverse price movement forces repeated margin calls faster than the holder can raise cash. During stress, the interaction between leverage and funding can amplify losses across the system, especially when many participants are trying to meet the same calls at the same time [1][34].

For that reason, margin should be analyzed as a dynamic liquidity requirement, not merely as a percentage of notional. The relevant questions are how quickly the margin can rise, what assets are eligible, whether those assets are themselves correlated with the trade, and how procyclical the margin methodology is under stress. If the collateral pool consists of the same asset class that is declining in value, the trader is effectively posting weaker support precisely when support is most needed. This is one reason collateral policy matters at the portfolio level: cash, Treasuries, high-quality sovereigns, and carefully controlled substitutes have very different resilience characteristics. A margin system that appears prudent in calm markets can become destabilizing if it forces asset sales into a falling market, a mechanism that has been central to many financial dislocations [4][47].

Collateral management is therefore the operational layer that determines whether margining works in practice. It is not enough to post collateral; the book must know where it is, how it is segregated, what haircuts apply, how often it is revalued, and how quickly it can be substituted or recalled. Collateral is also a balance-sheet resource, which means it is scarce even when nominally abundant. A dealer may have ample assets but still face bottlenecks if those assets are trapped in the wrong legal entity, pledged elsewhere, or unavailable in the needed currency. A risk manager should think of collateral as a chain of dependencies: instrument valuation, exposure measurement, margin calculation, collateral eligibility, settlement timing, and dispute resolution. Weakness at any link can turn a manageable market move into an operational failure.

The most serious errors arise when firms treat counterparty, margin, and collateral issues as separate functions rather than one integrated control problem. A concentrated derivatives book can show low VaR, attractive carry, and apparently modest Greeks while still carrying unacceptable wrong-way risk if the counterparty weakens as the trade moves against it. Systemic stress tends to expose these linkages because market liquidity, dealer balance-sheet capacity, and funding conditions deteriorate together. Research on intermediary constraints and systemic spillovers reinforces the point that the health of the counterparty network matters as much as the standalone risk of the position [45][160]. In that environment, the quality of the trade is determined not only by the payoff profile but by whether the exposure can be margined, collateralized, and closed out under adverse conditions without forcing the portfolio into a fire sale.

That is why professional derivatives practice increasingly distinguishes between economic exposure and survivable exposure. A trade may be economically attractive but operationally unacceptable if the collateral terms are too loose, the margin model too procyclical, or the counterparty too closely tied to the same stress factor being hedged. The discipline is to size positions so that even a severe move, combined with delayed collateral settlement and temporary market illiquidity, does not jeopardize the broader portfolio. In derivatives, the contract is only the first layer of risk. The second layer is the funding and credit infrastructure that keeps the contract alive long enough for the hedge or strategy to work.

Governance, controls, and post-trade risk review processes

Governance is what turns derivatives activity from a collection of independent trades into a controlled business process. In a professional setting, the question is not only whether a position is attractive, but whether it has been approved through the right authority, booked in the right system, valued by the right methodology, and monitored against limits that reflect the firm's actual risk appetite. That discipline matters because derivatives can create exposures that are larger, more path-dependent, and more operationally fragile than their initial premium or margin requirement suggests. When governance is weak, the failure is often not a single bad trade but a chain of small breakdowns: a mandate that was too vague, a limit that was too easy to override, a valuation that was accepted without challenge, or a confirmation that was never reconciled to the executed terms.

A credible control framework begins before execution. Trade approval should be tied to a documented strategy objective, an approved universe of instruments, and a clearly defined risk budget. For a trading desk, that usually means separating the person generating the idea from the person authorizing the exposure and from the function that independently verifies the economics. This separation is not bureaucratic overhead; it is the mechanism that prevents a position from being justified only by the optimism of the trader who wants to hold it. The approval record should identify why the trade fits the mandate, what risks it introduces, how it will be hedged or monitored, and what conditions would trigger reduction or exit. In institutions with multiple portfolios, the same trade may be acceptable in one account and prohibited in another simply because of liquidity, leverage, tax, or benchmark constraints. Governance has to preserve those distinctions rather than flatten them into a generic yes-or-no process.

Pre-trade controls are most effective when they are embedded in systems rather than left to manual judgment. Hard limits on notional exposure, Greeks, tenor, concentration, and counterparty usage can prevent a single order from exceeding policy even if the trader is under pressure to act quickly. More refined controls also test whether the trade would breach scenario-based thresholds, such as a defined loss under a gap move, a volatility shock, or a correlation break. The point is not to eliminate discretion, because many derivatives trades require judgment about timing and structure. The point is to force discretion to operate inside a framework that already knows where the firm is willing to absorb risk and where it is not. This becomes especially important in options portfolios, where a position can look modest in premium terms while carrying significant convexity or short-volatility exposure.

Post-trade controls should be built around independent verification rather than simple recordkeeping. Confirmations, allocations, lifecycle events, and corporate actions all need to be matched against the executed terms, because even a small mismatch in strike, expiry, quantity, or settlement convention can materially alter the economics of the book. Independent valuation is equally important. For liquid listed contracts, market marks are often straightforward, but for OTC structures, thinly traded options, or bespoke overlays, the price used for risk reporting can depend on model inputs, curve construction, and liquidity adjustments. That is why valuation control functions need authority to challenge marks, request supporting evidence, and escalate disputes when the economics do not reconcile cleanly. In markets where information is incomplete or rapidly changing, the quality of the control process is often more important than the elegance of the pricing model [10].

Post-trade risk review is where the firm tests whether the position still makes sense after the market has moved, time has passed, or the original thesis has weakened. A useful review process does not ask only whether the trade is profitable; it asks whether the position is behaving as expected relative to the assumptions that justified it. If a volatility trade was entered because implied volatility appeared rich to realized volatility, the review should examine whether the spread is narrowing, whether the hedge is functioning, and whether the book has accumulated unwanted directional exposure through rebalancing costs or skew shifts. If a spread was structured to cap loss, the review should verify that the cap still holds under current conditions and that the residual tail risk remains within policy. The review should also compare realized behavior against pre-trade scenario analysis so that the desk learns not just from gains and losses, but from the accuracy of its risk framing.

That learning function matters because derivatives markets are not static systems. Pricing assumptions, liquidity conditions, and even the interpretation of risk can evolve as participants update their beliefs. Research on learning in financial markets emphasizes that model parameters are uncertain and subject to revision [232], which is directly relevant to derivatives oversight: a control framework that assumes yesterday's vol surface, correlation regime, or funding condition will remain stable is vulnerable to surprise. A robust review process therefore records not just P&L, but the state variables that drove it, the hedges that were used, the slippage incurred, and the reasons any exceptions were granted. Over time, those records make it possible to distinguish between a strategy that was structurally sound but poorly executed and one whose apparent edge was really a hidden form of risk-taking.

Effective governance also requires escalation rules that are specific enough to be actionable. A desk should know when a mark dispute becomes a model review, when a limit breach becomes a management issue, and when repeated exceptions indicate a policy failure rather than a temporary market anomaly. The same applies to concentration and counterparty usage. Derivatives can transmit stress quickly through interconnected positions, and episodes of contagion show that adverse shocks do not remain isolated when exposures are linked across institutions and instruments [8]. That means post-trade review has to extend beyond the individual ticket to the portfolio and counterparty network: which positions are correlated, which hedges depend on the same liquidity source, and which settlements would become problematic if a single dealer or clearing relationship were disrupted. In periods of stress, loss of information about where risk resides can be as damaging as the risk itself [10].

At the highest level, the purpose of controls is not to suppress trading but to make trading auditable, repeatable, and survivable. A firm that can explain why a derivative was entered, how it was approved, how it was valued, how it was hedged, and how it was reviewed is far better positioned than one that relies on informal memory or post hoc justification. That discipline becomes especially important when incentives encourage risk-taking without equally strong checks on the quality of the process. Governance is therefore not a separate administrative layer; it is part of the economics of the trade itself, because the expected value of a derivatives strategy depends not only on market conditions, but on whether the organization can actually monitor, control, and learn from the exposure it has created.

CHAPTER 10

Chapter 10: Real-World Applications Across Markets and Industries

Once derivatives move out of the abstract and into operating portfolios, their value is judged by how well they translate broad market exposure into something that can be measured, hedged, and governed inside a real institution. The same instrument can serve very different purposes depending on whether it is being used to reduce unwanted risk, preserve strategic exposure, or align a portfolio with a liability, budget, or cash-flow constraint. That is why real-world application matters: the contract itself is only the starting point, and the practical question is how it behaves when embedded in a mandate, a balance sheet, or a trading process.

Equity hedging and event-driven positioning

Equity hedging is usually introduced as a way to reduce downside, but in practice it is a way to control which downside matters, when it matters, and how much capital is committed to defending it. A portfolio manager with a long equity book is rarely trying to eliminate market exposure outright. More often the objective is to preserve strategic ownership while reducing the sensitivity to a known vulnerability: a macro event, an earnings season, a policy announcement, a liquidity shock, or a period in which correlations tend to rise and passive diversification weakens. The hedge is therefore not an abstract insurance policy. It is a selective transfer of risk away from the part of the equity book that is least tolerable under a particular scenario.

The first decision is whether the hedge should be static or dynamic. A static hedge, such as buying index puts or structuring a collar, accepts some premium cost in exchange for a clearly defined floor. That approach is attractive when the primary concern is a discrete drawdown window and the portfolio must remain invested without frequent intervention. A dynamic hedge, by contrast, uses futures, index options, or sector overlays to adjust exposure as market conditions change. Dynamic hedging can be more capital efficient, but it also depends on execution, liquidity, and the trader's ability to rebalance without turning the hedge itself into a source of slippage. In stressed markets, that distinction becomes critical because the hedge must be tradable when its protection is most needed, not merely cheap when conditions are calm [1][4].

For institutional books, the choice of instrument is often driven by the shape of the risk rather than the direction of the view. Index futures are efficient for broad beta reduction, but they leave the portfolio exposed to idiosyncratic names and factor tilts. Put options provide convex protection, but the premium can be expensive if the market is already pricing elevated uncertainty. Put spreads can reduce that cost by financing part of the hedge, though they cap the benefit beyond the lower strike. Collars exchange some upside for downside protection and are often used when a portfolio must remain invested but cannot tolerate a large gap lower. The relevant question is not which structure is "best," but which one matches the portfolio's loss profile, liquidity profile, and governance limits.

Event-driven positioning uses the same toolkit, but the risk being managed is narrower and more time-specific. The market may face an earnings release, a merger vote, a regulatory decision, a product launch, a litigation milestone, an index rebalance, or a central bank meeting that can reprice the underlying in a matter of minutes. In these settings, options are often preferred because they isolate the event window while limiting capital at risk to the premium paid. A trader may buy a straddle ahead of an announcement when the expected move is believed to exceed the implied move embedded in the options, or may sell premium when the market appears to have overpaid for event uncertainty. The essential point is that event-driven positioning is not simply a directional forecast; it is a forecast about the distribution of outcomes around a known catalyst.

That distribution matters because event risk is often asymmetric. An earnings release can produce a modest move in either direction most of the time, but occasionally create a discontinuous repricing if guidance, margins, or forward demand surprise the market. A merger announcement may compress volatility if the deal is viewed as certain, yet explode if antitrust concerns or financing risk re-enter the price. In such cases, the option market is often pricing not just the expected move but the market's fear of being wrong. Implied volatility around the event becomes a compact summary of that uncertainty, and the trader's task is to decide whether the premium reflects a fair transfer of risk or an overpayment for protection.

Event-driven positioning also requires attention to path dependence. A hedge or speculative option position can be correct on the event itself and still lose money if it is entered too late, rolled too aggressively, or sized without regard to the surrounding term structure. Short-dated options can decay rapidly into the catalyst, and the premium may collapse immediately after the announcement even if the move is directionally favorable. Longer-dated options may retain more flexibility but can dilute the event-specific edge. This is why experienced traders often separate the event thesis from the holding-period thesis: the first concerns the catalyst, while the second concerns how long the market will continue to reprice the information after it arrives.

There is also a portfolio-level dimension that is easy to overlook. Equity hedging and event-driven positioning do not only affect P&L; they affect liquidity, margin, and the firm's ability to respond to new information. A hedge that looks efficient in isolation may consume too much capital when volatility rises, while an event trade that seems small may create operational strain if several positions are exposed to the same catalyst. CoVaR-style thinking is useful here because it emphasizes the contribution of one position to the risk of the broader book under stress, rather than its standalone variance [160]. In the same spirit, the liquidity conditions that emerge during market stress can make hedges more expensive to enter or unwind precisely when the desk most wants flexibility [1][234].

For this reason, the best equity hedges and event structures are designed with both the market and the institution in mind. The market question is whether the option premium, forward curve, or futures basis offers favorable terms for transferring the risk. The institutional question is whether the position can be monitored, adjusted, and exited under the firm's actual constraints. A hedge that cannot be rolled, a catalyst trade that cannot be scaled, or a protection structure that fails under a volatility spike is not a hedge in the practical sense. It is simply another exposure whose risk has been renamed.

Interest rate and fixed-income derivatives in portfolio management

Interest rate derivatives sit at the center of portfolio management because they translate a manager's view on funding, policy, inflation, and curve shape into instruments that can be sized and controlled with far more precision than cash bonds alone. A portfolio that holds fixed-income assets is never just exposed to "rates" in the abstract; it is exposed to level, slope, curvature, convexity, reinvestment risk, and the financing terms that govern how those exposures are carried. Futures, swaps, swaptions, caps, floors, and Treasury options each isolate a different part of that risk budget. The practical question is not which instrument is most sophisticated, but which one best matches the portfolio's objective: reducing duration, expressing a view on the yield curve, protecting liability values, or transforming a static bond book into a more adaptable risk engine.

For many institutional portfolios, the first use of rate derivatives is duration management. A bond portfolio can be shortened or lengthened without liquidating the underlying holdings by using Treasury futures or interest rate swaps, which allows the manager to preserve credit exposure, tax positioning, or portfolio composition while adjusting sensitivity to rate moves. This matters because the cash bond market is often ill-suited to rapid reconfiguration. If a manager expects policy tightening, for example, the book can be reduced in duration with a payer swap or a short futures overlay rather than by selling a large block of bonds into a potentially unfavorable market. Conversely, if liabilities extend far into the future, receiver swaps can increase duration efficiently and with lower transaction costs than buying long-dated cash bonds in size.

Curve positioning is a more refined application. The yield curve does not move as a single object; it twists, steepens, flattens, and sometimes dislocates across tenors in response to growth, inflation, supply, and central bank expectations. A portfolio manager who uses only parallel-shift intuition will miss a large part of the risk embedded in the book. Rate derivatives allow the manager to express or hedge those non-parallel moves with much greater specificity. A steepener or flattener trade can be implemented through futures across maturities or through swap exposure at different points on the curve. That precision is valuable in portfolios where the objective is not to guess the absolute level of rates, but to isolate the spread between short and long maturities or the relative value between nominal and inflation-linked instruments.

Swaps are especially important because they convert balance-sheet and funding considerations into tradable rate exposure. In a plain fixed-for-floating swap, the portfolio can exchange one stream of cash flows for another, which changes the effective interest rate profile without changing the underlying asset base. This is why swaps are central in liability-driven investing and in fixed-income mandates that must manage long-dated obligations. The swap market also allows a manager to separate credit risk from interest rate risk. A corporate bond portfolio, for instance, may retain spread exposure while hedging a portion of its duration with swaps, thereby targeting the source of return that is actually intended. The same logic applies to mortgage portfolios, structured credit books, and insurers that need to align asset duration with liability duration while preserving spread income.

Options on rates add another layer of control because they convert uncertainty into asymmetric protection. A cap can protect against rising floating-rate costs, a floor can preserve minimum reinvestment income, and a swaption can preserve the right, but not the obligation, to enter a swap if rates move in an unfavorable direction. These instruments are particularly useful when the portfolio's concern is not a single forecast, but a distribution of outcomes. A manager may not know whether rates will rise immediately, drift sideways, or fall first and rise later, but can still structure protection around the risk that matters most. That is especially relevant in environments where policy uncertainty is high and rate volatility itself becomes a portfolio variable. The option premium is the cost of buying flexibility, and in fixed income that flexibility often has direct economic value because it preserves the ability to respond after the macro regime has become clearer.

Fixed-income derivatives are also indispensable in liability management, where the portfolio is judged against obligations rather than against a benchmark alone. Pension funds, insurers, and endowments with long-dated commitments use rate derivatives to align asset sensitivity with liability sensitivity, reducing the risk that a fall in discount rates inflates present-value obligations faster than the asset base can respond. In that setting, the derivative is not a speculative overlay but a structural tool for stabilizing funded status. The relevant risk measure is often not mark-to-market volatility in isolation, but the mismatch between asset and liability duration, curve exposure, and convexity. Because those liabilities may react differently to shifts at the front end, belly, or long end of the curve, derivative overlays are often built in slices rather than as a single blunt hedge.

There are, however, important implementation constraints. Fixed-income derivatives are highly sensitive to collateral terms, margin flows, and the liquidity of the underlying hedge instruments. During stressed periods, funding conditions can dominate the economics of an apparently well-designed rate position, and a hedge that is effective in theory may be difficult to maintain if variation margin demands arrive faster than liquidity can be raised. Model assumptions also matter because the valuation of swaps, options, and futures depends on discounting conventions, curve construction, and volatility surfaces that may shift materially when markets reprice. This is one reason model uncertainty is not a theoretical nuisance but a live risk factor in derivative portfolios [198].

For portfolio management, the main value of interest rate and fixed-income derivatives is that they permit the manager to decompose a bond book into its underlying drivers and then rebuild the exposure in a more deliberate form. Duration can be resized, curve shape can be targeted, convexity can be purchased or sold, and liability risk can be matched without forcing wholesale turnover in the cash portfolio. That flexibility is powerful precisely because it is selective: it lets the manager decide which parts of fixed-income exposure are strategic and which are merely incidental. In practice, that selectivity is what turns rate derivatives from trading instruments into portfolio architecture.

Commodity and energy hedging for producers, consumers, and traders

Commodity and energy hedging is where derivatives move from abstract risk transfer into the operating realities of production, processing, storage, transport, and consumption. In these markets, the exposure is rarely a simple directional view on price. A producer may care about the margin between extraction cost and realized sale price, a consumer may care about input cost stability, and a trader may care about basis, timing, and inventory optionality. The hedging problem is therefore operational as much as financial. Research on the operations-finance interface emphasizes that material flows, cash flows, and information flows have to be managed together when uncertainty is high [74]. In commodities, that integration is not a theoretical preference; it is the condition for making a hedge economically meaningful.

For producers, the central objective is usually to protect revenue without destroying the upside embedded in the asset base. An oil producer, a grain elevator, or a metal miner may use futures, swaps, or option structures to lock in a portion of expected output at acceptable levels. The hedge ratio is rarely one-to-one with physical production, because output volumes are uncertain, grades vary, and timing rarely matches the standardized contract schedule. A producer may layer hedges across delivery months, use a strip rather than a single contract, and leave part of the position unhedged to preserve flexibility if production falls short or if prices rally sharply. Options are especially useful when the producer wants floor protection without giving up all upside. A put establishes a minimum sale price net of premium, while a collar can reduce or eliminate that premium cost by financing the put with a call sale. The choice is not merely about price direction; it is about how much cash flow certainty the business requires and how much participation it can afford to forgo.

Consumers face the mirror image of the same problem. A refinery, airline, utility, food processor, or industrial manufacturer is often exposed to input costs that can move faster than output prices, compressing margins even when demand remains stable. Hedging in this context is less about making a speculative call and more about stabilizing the spread between input cost and finished-product revenue. An airline may hedge jet fuel, but the real economic exposure is the fuel bill relative to ticket pricing and load factors. A food processor may hedge corn, wheat, or edible oils, but the real concern is the conversion margin between raw inputs and finished goods. This is why commodity hedging often involves a portfolio of instruments rather than a single contract. Futures can lock in price, options can preserve benefit from favorable moves, and swaps can align longer-dated cost expectations with budgeting cycles. In markets with pronounced seasonality or event risk, the hedge itself may need to be staged so that it does not create a new concentration at a single expiration.

Basis risk is one of the defining complications in commodity and energy hedging. The physical commodity being produced or consumed is often not the same thing as the exchange-traded reference contract. Location, grade, quality, delivery point, transportation constraint, and timing all affect the relationship between the hedge instrument and the cash market. A natural gas producer in one basin may hedge with a benchmark contract that does not perfectly track realized regional pricing. A power generator may face spark spread exposure rather than outright fuel exposure. A grain merchant may need to manage the spread between local elevator prices and a national futures benchmark. The hedge can still be effective, but only if the mismatch is measured and accepted as part of the risk budget. In practice, basis risk is not a nuisance variable; it is often the dominant source of residual P&L after the directional exposure has been neutralized.

Energy markets add another layer because the underlying economics are shaped by storage, transportation, dispatch, and physical constraints. Electricity, in particular, behaves differently from storable commodities because supply and demand must balance continuously, and price spikes can emerge when the system is short of available capacity. The deregulation of electricity markets increased the need for derivative products that protect against price spikes and volatility in power prices [236][240]. For generators and large consumers, the relevant hedge may involve forward power strips, spark spreads, heat rate structures, or options on peak and off-peak prices. These instruments are designed to reflect the fact that electricity value is not just a function of fuel cost; it is also a function of congestion, weather, outage risk, and the inability to store large quantities economically. A power hedge that ignores those features may reduce headline price risk while leaving the business exposed to the very conditions that matter most.

Traders occupy a different role because they are not simply transferring risk away from the balance sheet; they are often warehousing, transforming, or arbitraging it. An agricultural merchant may hold inventory, hedge it in futures, and use the spread between physical and paper markets to manage timing and quality optionality. An energy merchant may exploit storage economics, location differentials, and seasonal curve structure. In these businesses, the derivative book is inseparable from logistics and financing. The trader's edge often comes from understanding how the hedge interacts with inventory turns, storage capacity, transportation bottlenecks, and counterparty terms. Commodity trading firms have long used these networked relationships to support hedging and profit generation simultaneously [239]. That dual use of derivatives is powerful, but it requires discipline: a hedge intended to neutralize risk can become a speculative position if the physical assumptions change faster than the financial book is adjusted.

Recent market history also shows that commodity hedging cannot be evaluated only by average conditions. Food and energy prices can experience extreme spikes, policy intervention, and abrupt changes in correlation structure [237][238]. Inflationary pressure can propagate through energy and food channels simultaneously, forcing producers and consumers to hedge not just price levels but the volatility of the broader cost environment [63][237]. Carbon markets add yet another dimension, where compliance obligations, regulatory changes, and industrial output shifts all affect the value of allowances and offsets [200]. In these settings, the hedge must be stress-tested under scenarios where liquidity thins, margins rise, and the cash business itself is under pressure. A derivative that looks efficient in a stable market may be inadequate when the operating business most needs protection. That is why commodity and energy hedging is best treated as a continuous governance process: aligning contract tenor with physical exposure, monitoring basis and volume risk, and revising the hedge as production plans, demand forecasts, and market structure evolve.

FX and cross-border exposure management in global operations

Foreign exchange exposure is rarely confined to the treasury desk. In a global operating model, it enters through sales invoices, procurement contracts, intercompany funding, royalty streams, cross-border payroll, foreign subsidiaries, and the translation of overseas earnings back into the reporting currency. The first task is to separate transaction exposure from translation exposure and economic exposure, because each responds to a different hedge design. Transaction exposure is the most immediate: a receivable, payable, or debt obligation denominated in a foreign currency creates a known cash-flow uncertainty between trade date and settlement. Translation exposure arises when the balance sheets and income statements of foreign entities must be consolidated into the parent's reporting currency. Economic exposure is broader still, affecting the competitive position of the firm through pricing power, margin structure, and the currency composition of costs and revenues over time.

For transaction exposure, the simplest hedge is often the most effective: a forward contract, swap, or money market hedge that locks in the domestic-currency value of a future foreign-currency cash flow. But operational simplicity should not be mistaken for strategic completeness. A firm with recurring exposures in multiple currencies may need a layered program that matches hedge tenor to the business cycle, aligns notional amounts with forecast confidence, and distinguishes highly probable cash flows from contingent ones. If the forecast itself is unstable, over-hedging can create speculative risk rather than reduce it. That is why treasury policy usually defines hedge ratios by exposure class, horizon, and probability of occurrence, rather than applying a single blanket percentage to all foreign-currency items.

Options become especially useful when the cash flow is uncertain in timing or magnitude, or when management wants protection without surrendering all favorable currency movement. A call on the domestic currency or a put on the foreign currency can establish a floor for a foreign-currency inflow while preserving upside if the foreign currency strengthens. The premium paid is the price of that flexibility, and in practice the decision often turns on whether the exposure is budget-sensitive or margin-sensitive. If a firm must protect a minimum dollar value to preserve covenant headroom or project economics, option-based hedging can be appropriate even when forwards appear cheaper. If the exposure is highly certain and the firm is indifferent to favorable moves, a forward may be more efficient. The choice is not merely about cost; it is about how much variability the business can absorb before the currency move becomes an operating problem.

Cross-border operations also face a structural issue that is easy to underestimate: currency risk is often coupled with funding risk. A subsidiary may borrow in local currency to match local assets, but the parent may still face upstreaming constraints, capital controls, or refinancing risk if local markets tighten. In periods of stress, access to dollar funding can become a system-wide constraint, especially for institutions with large offshore balance sheets and short-term liabilities. Central bank swap lines were designed in part to reduce that ex post financing risk by improving foreign-currency liquidity backstops for banks operating across jurisdictions [242]. For corporate treasuries, the lesson is narrower but important: a hedge that looks complete on a mark-to-market basis may still fail to protect the business if the relevant currency cannot be funded, rolled, or repatriated when needed.

Hedging policy therefore has to be integrated with the organization's capital structure, legal entity map, and operational footprint. A multinational may choose to leave some foreign earnings unhedged at the operating level if those cash flows are naturally reinvested abroad, while hedging the translation effect only at the consolidated reporting level. Another firm may prefer to hedge net investments in foreign subsidiaries to stabilize book value or debt metrics. The right answer depends on whether the business is optimizing reported earnings, cash flow stability, covenant protection, or economic competitiveness. Research on firm behavior under policy uncertainty suggests that firms do adjust foreign direct investment and hedging choices when home and host-country uncertainty diverge [241], which is consistent with the broader observation that currency risk management is inseparable from the geography of real operations.

In practice, the most robust FX programs are built around exposure netting and selective layering rather than constant full coverage. Natural hedges, such as matching local costs with local revenues or borrowing in the same currency as the asset base, can reduce the amount of derivative hedging required. Intercompany netting can compress gross exposures before they reach the market. Layered hedging can then be used to add coverage progressively as forecast certainty improves, avoiding the trap of locking in a rate too early on exposures that may never materialize. This approach is particularly useful for firms with seasonal sales, project-based procurement, or long lead times, because it preserves flexibility while still constraining adverse moves within a tolerable band.

The derivative book itself should be monitored as a source of operational and governance risk, not just market risk. FX hedges can create basis risk when the hedged cash flow and the hedge instrument reference different currencies, fixing dates, or valuation conventions. They can create accounting volatility if hedge documentation, effectiveness testing, or designation rules are not aligned with the economic purpose of the trade. They can also create concentration risk if a treasury desk repeatedly hedges only the most visible exposures while ignoring smaller but persistent currency drifts embedded in working capital, intercompany balances, and procurement contracts. For global operations, the most effective currency management framework is one that treats FX not as a standalone trading problem, but as a recurring translation layer between the firm's commercial reality and its reporting currency.

CHAPTER 11

Chapter 11: Regulation, Ethics, and the Future of Derivatives Innovation

As derivatives become more embedded in capital formation, risk transfer, and market plumbing, the boundary between innovation and fragility becomes harder to see in real time. Regulation, ethics, and market design therefore cannot be treated as external constraints added after the fact; they shape what products can be trusted, how exposures are governed, and whether complexity serves a legitimate economic purpose or merely obscures it. The post-crisis regulatory environment reflects that tension, as markets have been pushed toward greater transparency and control even while product design, execution technology, and distribution channels continue to evolve [225][38].

Key regulatory themes: reporting, clearing, margin, and disclosure

Reporting is the first line of regulatory control because it converts a bilateral or market-wide derivatives book into something visible to supervisors, counterparties, and internal governance functions. In practice, the key issue is not simply whether a trade was booked, but whether it was reported accurately, on time, and in a form that allows the transaction to be reconstructed after the fact. That includes product classification, notional amount, maturity, counterparty identity, execution venue, and lifecycle events such as novations, compressions, resets, terminations, and collateral changes. For large institutions, reporting is as much an operational discipline as a compliance requirement: a trade that is economically correct but misclassified can distort position limits, capital calculations, and exposure aggregation. The post-crisis regulatory architecture was built in part to reduce the opacity that had characterized OTC derivatives markets, where hidden interconnectedness had amplified systemic stress [210][252].

Clearing changes the risk profile of a derivatives contract by replacing direct bilateral exposure with exposure to a central counterparty, but that shift is only beneficial if the clearing model is understood in its full economic context. Central clearing reduces counterparty concentration and creates a standardized process for margining, default management, and netting, which can make large books more manageable and more transparent. At the same time, it concentrates risk in the clearinghouse itself and imposes operational demands on members and clients who must meet variation margin calls, manage eligible collateral, and maintain access to liquidity under stressed conditions. This matters especially in markets where financing and maturity transformation already depend on fragile funding structures, because the apparent safety of central clearing can be offset by liquidity pressure elsewhere in the system [248][210][253]. For practitioners, the question is not whether clearing is good or bad in the abstract, but whether the instrument, liquidity profile, and portfolio purpose make central clearing an efficient transfer of risk or merely a different location for it.

Margin is the mechanism that turns abstract exposure into a daily funding requirement. Initial margin is intended to cover potential future exposure over a liquidation horizon, while variation margin reflects current mark-to-market losses and gains as they accrue. That distinction is crucial because a position can be economically sound and still fail if the holder cannot meet margin calls during a drawdown or volatility spike. In derivatives, liquidity risk often arrives before solvency risk: a portfolio may still have positive long-run value, but if collateral must be posted quickly, the trader may be forced to reduce exposure at unfavorable prices. This is one reason why margin policy cannot be separated from strategy design. A structure that looks efficient on a model sheet may be unacceptable if it creates large procyclical funding needs, especially in stressed markets where collateral haircuts rise and funding spreads widen. The regulatory emphasis on margin is therefore not merely protective; it is an attempt to force the market to internalize the liquidity cost of leverage before that cost becomes a systemic event [164][210].

For OTC derivatives, margin and clearing interact with collateral management in ways that are easy to underestimate. Bilateral agreements may allow more customization, but they also require careful attention to thresholds, minimum transfer amounts, eligible collateral schedules, dispute resolution, and the timing of margin calls. These details matter because the contract's legal economics and its funding economics are inseparable. A swap or option overlay that appears hedge-like can become a source of cash drain if the collateral terms are tight or the market moves sharply against the position. Central clearing simplifies some of that complexity, but it does not eliminate the need to manage collateral quality, concentration, and liquidity. The broader lesson is that leverage in derivatives is never just a question of notional size; it is a question of how quickly losses translate into cash obligations and how resilient the funding base is when multiple counterparties are demanding protection at once [248][253].

Disclosure is the regulatory theme that ties the others together, because it determines what investors, clients, counterparties, and boards are actually told about the risks being taken. In a professional setting, disclosure should not be reduced to a legal formality or a boilerplate product description. It should explain the economic logic of the position, the circumstances under which the payoff can deteriorate, the embedded optionality or path dependence, and the ways in which liquidity, margin, and counterparty conditions can alter realized outcomes. This is especially important for structured products, complex overlays, and OTC trades sold into less sophisticated accounts, where the gap between headline yield and embedded risk can be substantial. The regulatory concern is not merely that investors may dislike a loss; it is that they may not understand which risk they are being paid to bear. Suitability and disclosure standards therefore function as a check on asymmetry of information, particularly when derivatives are distributed through intermediaries, wrapped in notes, or marketed as conservative alternatives to direct exposure [250][252].

A mature derivatives program treats reporting, clearing, margin, and disclosure as a single control system rather than four separate compliance boxes. Reporting makes the book visible, clearing determines where credit risk resides, margin determines how that risk is funded, and disclosure determines whether the economic terms are understood by the people who approve, buy, or supervise the trade. Weakness in any one of these areas can undermine the others. A position that is properly cleared but poorly reported may still escape internal limits; a trade that is fully disclosed but under-margined may still create a funding shock; a structure that is compliant on paper may still be mis-sold if its risks are not communicated plainly. For that reason, the best institutions do not treat regulatory obligations as an afterthought to trading. They build them into product approval, documentation, valuation, and post-trade review so that the legal architecture and the risk architecture reinforce one another rather than conflict [210][252].

Compliance risks, suitability, and fiduciary considerations

Compliance risk in derivatives is rarely a matter of one dramatic violation. More often it arises from small mismatches between what a desk thinks it traded, what the documentation actually permits, what the surveillance system records, and what the firm is allowed to recommend or hold under its policies. A trade can be economically rational and still be operationally or legally defective if it bypasses approval thresholds, exceeds mandate language, or is booked in a way that obscures the true exposure. In large institutions, the problem is amplified by product convergence: instruments that are economically similar may sit in different legal categories, clearing regimes, or disclosure frameworks, and financial markets increasingly bypass the traditional business lines that once made oversight simpler [258].

For that reason, compliance is not just a post-trade review function. It begins with product governance, counterparty onboarding, and the classification of the transaction itself. Listed options, OTC swaps, structured notes, and bespoke overlays may all serve hedging or return-seeking purposes, but each can trigger different obligations around reporting, margining, suitability review, and internal authorization. A desk that treats these distinctions as administrative detail can create regulatory exposure even when the market risk is well controlled. The same trade may also be subject to multiple internal rules at once: concentration limits, prohibited-asset screens, leverage caps, liquidity thresholds, and pre-trade approval requirements tied to the mandate or client agreement.

Suitability is the point at which the economic logic of a derivative meets the client's actual circumstances. A strategy that is theoretically efficient can still be unsuitable if it depends on constant monitoring, tolerance for large interim losses, or an understanding of path-dependent payoff behavior that the client does not possess. This matters especially in advisory and discretionary contexts, where the recommendation is judged not only by expected return but by whether the product fits the client's objectives, risk tolerance, experience, and ability to absorb adverse outcomes. The issue is not confined to retail distribution. Institutional accounts, pensions, endowments, and insurance portfolios can also be mismatched with derivative structures if the position creates accounting volatility, collateral strain, or governance burdens inconsistent with the mandate [259][260].

That is why documentation and disclosure are part of the investment decision itself. A trader may understand that a short option position carries convex loss, but the client or investment committee may focus on premium collected and underestimate the tail. A structured overlay may appear to reduce drawdown risk while actually introducing barrier features, autocall risk, or liquidity dependence that are not obvious from headline terms. Disclosure must therefore be specific enough to describe not only the instrument, but the circumstances under which the payoff changes character. In practice, the most dangerous suitability failures occur when a product is marketed as conservative, income-generating, or hedging-oriented while the embedded risks are concentrated in stress states that are least visible during calm markets.

Fiduciary considerations add another layer of discipline because the decision-maker is not merely allowed to trade; the decision-maker is expected to act in the beneficiary's interest. That requires more than avoiding obvious conflicts. It requires evidence that the derivative was selected for a client-specific purpose, that costs and alternatives were compared, and that the position was sized and monitored in a way consistent with the client's long-term welfare. For pension and retirement-oriented mandates, the interaction between regulation, accounting, and asset-liability constraints can materially alter the optimal use of derivatives, since the portfolio may need to manage contributions, funding ratios, and balance-sheet volatility rather than simple mark-to-market return [259][260].

Conflicts of interest are especially important where the same firm advises, executes, finances, clears, or structures the product. A dealer may have an incentive to recommend a structure that is easier to warehouse, hedge, or distribute, even if a simpler instrument would better serve the client. Broker-dealer recommendations are therefore scrutinized not only for accuracy but for the incentives embedded in the compensation model and the recommendation process [262]. In derivatives, this conflict can be subtle: the firm may not be pushing a plainly unsuitable product, but rather one whose spread, financing terms, or embedded optionality is more profitable to sell than to buy. Fiduciary quality depends on whether those incentives are identified and controlled, not merely disclosed after the fact.

Climate and other long-horizon structural risks further complicate suitability and fiduciary judgment because they can alter the distribution of outcomes in ways that are not captured by short historical samples. Regulators have already emphasized that climate risk should be treated as a financial risk with implications for institutions, markets, and portfolio resilience [94]. For derivatives users, that means the suitability of a hedge or overlay cannot be evaluated solely on recent volatility. A commodity producer, an insurer, or a long-duration investor may face a hedge that appears effective under normal conditions but becomes less reliable if the underlying risk regime shifts, correlations change, or liquidity deteriorates. The fiduciary question is not whether the trade works in a backtest, but whether it remains defensible under foreseeable stress and within the client's governance capacity.

In practice, strong control frameworks reduce these risks by forcing a tighter link between mandate, trade rationale, and post-trade monitoring. That includes written investment guidelines, escalation rules for exceptions, independent review of complex structures, and periodic reassessment of whether the derivative still serves the original purpose. It also means documenting the logic of the hedge or strategy in terms that a committee, regulator, or beneficiary could reconstruct later. When derivatives are used well, they should make the portfolio's risk profile more intentional. When they are used poorly, they often reveal a deeper failure: the gap between what the institution was authorized to do, what it believed it was doing, and what the contract actually required it to bear.

Financial innovation in listed and OTC derivatives

Financial innovation in derivatives rarely arrives as a clean break from earlier instruments. More often it appears as a reconfiguration of familiar economic functions: shifting risk, improving funding flexibility, widening access to a payoff, or making a hedge more precise for a narrower class of exposures. Listed and OTC markets innovate differently because their constraints are different. Listed contracts tend to innovate through standardization, contract design, and the creation of new expirations, underlyings, or settlement conventions that can be cleared and scaled across many participants. OTC markets innovate through customization, where the economic problem is often too specific for an exchange-listed template and the structure must be tailored to a balance sheet, liability stream, or operating exposure. The result is not two separate worlds but two complementary channels through which the same basic derivatives logic is adapted to different institutional needs.

In listed markets, innovation is usually visible first in product architecture. Exchanges can create contracts tied to new benchmarks, sector baskets, volatility measures, rates, or commodity grades, and can refine contract size, tick value, and expiration frequency to improve usability. That matters because a contract is only useful if it can be traded in increments that match the user's exposure without creating excessive basis risk or unwanted residuals. Standardization also supports innovation in market access: smaller contract sizes, weekly expirations, and more granular strike intervals can make hedging and tactical positioning more precise, while still preserving the clearinghouse protections that make listed markets attractive to institutions. Financial innovation here is often incremental, but its cumulative effect can be large because it lowers the friction between a portfolio's actual risk and the instrument used to manage it.

OTC innovation is more flexible but also more dependent on documentation, collateral, and counterparty quality. A customized swap, option, or structured forward can be built around a path-dependent payoff, a particular barrier, a bespoke reset schedule, a commodity quality differential, or a funding profile that does not exist in listed form. This is especially important for institutions whose economic exposures are not well represented by a standardized market contract. An energy producer may need a hedge linked to a specific delivery point; a pension sponsor may need a swap structure matched to benefit outflows; a bank may need a derivative that transforms one stream of cash flows into another without disturbing the rest of the balance sheet. The innovation is not just in the payoff itself, but in the ability to align the derivative with the actual business problem rather than forcing the business problem to fit the contract.

That flexibility, however, comes with a familiar trade-off: the more tailored the structure, the more difficult it becomes to observe, price, and unwind under stress. OTC innovation can obscure embedded leverage, optionality, and path dependence if the transaction is judged only on its initial premium or carry. It can also shift risk into forms that are harder to aggregate at the portfolio or system level, especially when many bilateral contracts reference similar risk factors but are documented differently. Research on intermediary asset pricing underscores that the condition of dealers and other intermediaries matters for pricing across asset classes, not just in one corner of the market [45]. When dealer balance sheets are constrained, the market price of customization can rise quickly, and the apparent efficiency of a bespoke hedge may erode precisely when it is most needed.

Innovation in both listed and OTC markets also changes how risk is distributed across participants. A standard listed contract may make it easier for a pension fund, asset manager, or commodity user to express a view or hedge exposure, but the same contract can become a crowded risk transfer mechanism if many participants rush to the same strike, tenor, or maturity. OTC structures can reduce that crowding by tailoring the exposure, yet they can also concentrate idiosyncratic counterparty risk and collateral dependence in a way that is less visible until stress emerges. Studies of hedge fund return dynamics and systemic risk have shown that illiquidity and correlation can intensify losses when markets are under pressure [3][138]. That same logic applies to innovative derivatives: a structure that appears diversified in calm markets may become highly correlated with other positions once funding, volatility, and dealer capacity all tighten at the same time.

The most durable innovations are usually those that improve transparency without sacrificing economic usefulness. In listed markets, that means contract design that makes hedging and valuation more straightforward, while preserving liquidity and clearing. In OTC markets, it means stronger documentation standards, more consistent collateral terms, and structures that can be explained in plain economic terms even if their payoff is complex. Innovation becomes problematic when it is used primarily to disguise risk, reduce regulatory visibility, or manufacture an appearance of yield that depends on hidden convexity or unstable funding. The lesson from the evolution of modern financial economics is that models and contracts do not simply describe markets; they help build them, and the way they are implemented shapes behavior, liquidity, and risk transfer [24]. For that reason, the relevant question is not whether a derivative is new, but whether the innovation genuinely improves the allocation of risk, capital, and information.

The frontier between listed and OTC markets is also becoming more permeable. Exchange-traded products increasingly borrow features once associated with bespoke structures, while OTC markets increasingly reference standardized indices, benchmarks, and clearing conventions to reduce operational and counterparty friction. This convergence is important because it allows institutions to choose along a spectrum rather than between two rigid categories. A trader may use a listed option for core convexity, an OTC overlay for precise basis management, and a cleared swap for balance-sheet efficiency, all within the same risk program. Financial innovation, in that sense, is not a matter of inventing ever more exotic instruments. It is the ongoing refinement of how derivatives are packaged, distributed, collateralized, and integrated into portfolios so that risk can be transferred with more precision and less unintended damage than before.

Emerging trends: automation, tokenization, and market structure change

Automation is changing derivatives trading first at the level of process, then at the level of market behavior. What was once a sequence of discrete human judgments—screening opportunities, quoting prices, routing orders, hedging inventory, monitoring limits—has increasingly become a machine-mediated workflow in which models generate signals, execution engines stage orders, and surveillance systems flag anomalies in near real time. That shift matters because derivatives are especially sensitive to timing, and timing is exactly where automation creates both efficiency and new forms of fragility. A desk that automates strike selection or hedge rebalancing can respond faster to volatility changes, but it also inherits model risk at machine speed: a bad assumption, stale data feed, or unstable feedback loop can propagate across a book before human judgment catches up. Research on finance's technology frontier has emphasized that these systems are not merely incremental tools; they are part of a broader paradigm shift in how financial decisions are produced and coordinated [263][264].

In practice, automation is most valuable where the task is repetitive, rule-based, and latency-sensitive. Quote generation, volatility surface updates, scenario scanning, collateral calls, and intraday hedge adjustments are all natural candidates. The advantage is not only speed but consistency: a machine can apply the same rule across hundreds of strikes and expirations without fatigue or discretion drift. Yet the same consistency can become a liability when market conditions move outside the calibration range. Automated systems tend to encode yesterday's structure into today's response, which is acceptable in stable regimes and dangerous in discontinuous ones. For that reason, sophisticated derivatives operations increasingly separate decision automation from decision authority. The system may recommend, size, or stage a trade, but human oversight remains necessary for limit exceptions, event risk, and situations where liquidity is too thin for a purely mechanical response. The operations-finance interface literature is useful here because it frames risk management as coordination across material, monetary, and information flows rather than as a narrow pricing problem [74].

Automation also alters market structure by compressing the time between information and price. When many participants use similar signals, execution logic, and hedging triggers, the market can become more synchronized than diversified. That can improve displayed liquidity in normal conditions while making liquidity more conditional in stress. In derivatives, where a dealer's hedge in the underlying can feed back into the option price and a volatility shock can trigger further hedging, automation can amplify reflexivity. The issue is not that machines "cause" instability in isolation, but that they can intensify common responses across otherwise independent firms. This is especially relevant in options markets, where a change in implied volatility, open interest, or dealer gamma can provoke systematic rebalancing across multiple venues. A market structure built around speed and automation therefore demands stronger controls around throttles, kill switches, stale-quote detection, and pre-trade risk checks than a slower, more discretionary market would require.

Tokenization introduces a different kind of change. Instead of automating the workflow around traditional instruments, it attempts to redesign the instrument and its settlement layer. In tokenized systems, claims on assets or cash flows are represented on a distributed ledger, potentially allowing faster transfer, programmable restrictions, fractional ownership, and more granular collateral mobility. In principle, this can reduce operational friction and broaden access to exposures that were previously difficult to package or distribute. In practice, the central question is whether the token improves the economics of the derivative or merely repackages them in a new technical form. Studies of block-chain, digital money, and decentralized finance point to both the promise of new market architecture and the persistence of governance, legal, and liquidity challenges [263][209][265][172]. The technology can shorten settlement chains, but it does not eliminate the need for enforceable rights, reliable valuation, or clear recourse when something fails.

For derivatives, tokenization is most consequential when it affects collateral, margin, and post-trade portability. If a tokenized asset can move more quickly and transparently across counterparties, that may reduce funding friction and improve capital efficiency. If, however, the token's legal status is ambiguous, the smart contract is brittle, or the underlying reference asset cannot be cleanly linked to the on-chain representation, then the apparent efficiency may be illusory. The more complex the payoff, the more important it becomes that the tokenized structure map cleanly to enforceable economics. A simple cash claim is one thing; a path-dependent derivative with early exercise features, barrier conditions, or contingent settlement is another. Tokenization can support innovation, but it also raises the bar for documentation, auditability, and dispute resolution.

Market structure change is therefore not just about new technology; it is about the redistribution of functions across venues, protocols, and intermediaries. Listed exchanges, OTC dealers, clearinghouses, custodians, and now digital platforms each handle different parts of the lifecycle. As that architecture evolves, the most important question for derivatives users is where risk actually resides at each stage: before trade, at execution, during clearing, and through final settlement. In a more fragmented environment, price discovery may be spread across multiple venues while liquidity concentrates only intermittently. In a more automated environment, execution may be faster but less forgiving. In a more tokenized environment, transfer may be simpler but legal finality may become more nuanced. DeFi research highlights that systems offering lending, borrowing, and trading without traditional intermediaries can expand access, but they also face significant oversight and transaction-tracking challenges [209][265]. Those same tensions appear, in different form, whenever derivatives migrate toward programmable infrastructure.

The strategic implication for professional participants is that market structure can no longer be treated as a neutral backdrop. It is part of the trade. A model that ignores execution venue, settlement path, collateral mobility, or the behavior of automated counterparties is incomplete even if its pricing logic is sound. As financial innovation continues to merge software, market design, and contractual engineering, the edge will belong less to the participant who can merely identify a mispricing than to the one who understands how that mispricing survives contact with the actual plumbing of the market [74][263][264].

Citations

The following sources were referenced in the preceding chapters. Each entry links back to the inline reference in the text. All sources were verified against the OpenAlex academic database at the time of generation.

1. Markus K. Brunnermeier (2009). Deciphering the Liquidity and Credit Crunch 2007–2008. https://doi.org/10.1257/jep.23.1.77

2. Shaen Corbet, Brian M. Lucey, Andrew Urquhart et al. (2018). RETRACTED: Cryptocurrencies as a financial asset: A systematic analysis. https://doi.org/10.1016/j.irfa.2018.09.003

3. Mila Getmansky, Andrew W. Lo, Igor Makarov (2004). An econometric model of serial correlation and illiquidity in hedge fund returns. https://doi.org/10.1016/j.jfineco.2004.04.001

4. Markus K. Brunnermeier (2008). Deciphering the Liquidity and Credit Crunch 2007-08. https://doi.org/10.2139/ssrn.1317454

5. Louis O. Scott (1987). Option Pricing when the Variance Changes Randomly: Theory, Estimation, and an Application. https://doi.org/10.2307/2330793

6. Claudio Borio, Haibin Zhu (2008). Capital Regulation, Risk-Taking and Monetary Policy: A Missing Link in the Transmission Mechanism?. https://doi.org/10.2139/ssrn.1334132

7. Melanie Cao, V Akgiray, G Booth et al. (1988). Journal of international money and finance. https://doi.org/10.1016/0261-5606(88)90029-0

8. Graciela Kaminsky, Carmen Reinhart, Carlos Végh (2003). The Unholy Trinity of Financial Contagion. https://doi.org/10.1257/089533003772034899

9. Lieven Baele, Annalisa Ferrando, Peter Hördahl et al. (2004). Measuring financial integration in the euro area. https://openalex.org/W1495779368

10. Gary B. Gorton (2008). The Panic of 2007. https://doi.org/10.3386/w14358

11. John Watson, Mark McNaughton (2007). Gender Differences in Risk Aversion and Expected Retirement Benefits. https://doi.org/10.2469/faj.v63.n4.4749

12. Dylan Herman, Cody Googin, Xiaoyuan Liu et al. (2023). Quantum computing for finance. https://doi.org/10.1038/s42254-023-00603-1

13. Elizabeth Fuller Collins, David Hess, Cindy Maisannes et al. (2009). A Primer on Islamic Finance. https://doi.org/10.2470/rf.v2009.n6

14. Ana Njegovanović (2023). Financial Evolution and Interdisciplinary Research. https://doi.org/10.21272/fmir.7(1).71-95.2023

15. Eduardo A. Cavallo, Tomás Serebrisky, Verónica Frisancho et al. (2016). Saving for Development: How Latin America and the Caribbean Can Save More and Better. https://doi.org/10.18235/0012585

16. Douglas G. Baird (2017). Priority Matters: Absolute Priority, Relative Priority, and the Costs of Bankruptcy. https://openalex.org/W2617733937

17. William W. Jennings, Stephen M. Horan, William Reichenstein et al. (2010). Private Wealth Management: A Review. https://doi.org/10.2470/rflr.v5.n1.1

18. Ingo Walter, Robert D. Arnott, Theodore Aronson et al. (2015). The Industrial Organization of the Global Asset Management Business. https://doi.org/10.2470/rf.v2015.n5.1

19. J Derwall, N Gunster, R Bauer et al. (2017). Handbook on Sustainable Investments: Background Information and Practical Examples for Institutional Asset Owners. https://doi.org/10.2470/rf.v2017.n5.1

20. Rainer Beckmann, Wim Kösters, Jürgen Born (2001). The Us Dollar, the Euro, and the Yen: An Evaluation of Their Present and Future Status as International Currencies. https://doi.org/10.2139/ssrn.1698635

21. John R. Graham, Daniel A. Rogers (2002). Do Firms Hedge in Response to Tax Incentives?. https://doi.org/10.1111/1540-6261.00443

22. Xavier Gabaix, Matteo Maggiori (2015). International Liquidity and Exchange Rate Dynamics*. https://doi.org/10.1093/qje/qjv016

23. Robert DeYoung, Emma Y. Peng, Meng Yan (2013). Executive Compensation and Business Policy Choices at U.S. Commercial Banks. https://doi.org/10.1017/s0022109012000646

24. Donald MacKenzie (2003). An Equation and its Worlds. https://doi.org/10.1177/0306312703336002

25. Anat R. Admati, Peter M. DeMarzo, Martin Hellwig et al. (2013). Fallacies, Irrelevant Facts, and Myths in the Discussion of Capital Regulation: Why Bank Equity is Not Socially Expensive. https://doi.org/10.2139/ssrn.2349739

26. Xin Chang, Yangyang Chen, Sarah Qian Wang et al. (2019). Credit default swaps and corporate innovation. https://doi.org/10.1016/j.jfineco.2017.12.012

27. Frank Partnoy (1999). The Siskel and Ebert of Financial Markets?: Two Thumbs Down for the Credit Rating Agencies. https://openalex.org/W3125216888

28. Shihao Gu, Bryan Kelly, Dacheng Xiu (2020). Empirical Asset Pricing via Machine Learning. https://doi.org/10.1093/rfs/hhaa009

29. Robert J. Shiller (2003). From Efficient Markets Theory to Behavioral Finance. https://doi.org/10.1257/089533003321164967

30. Paul M. Healy, Krishna G. Palepu (2003). The Fall of Enron. https://doi.org/10.1257/089533003765888403

31. Robert J. Shiller (1990). Speculative Prices and Popular Models. https://doi.org/10.1257/jep.4.2.55

32. Fan Fang, Carmine Ventre, Michail Basios et al. (2022). Cryptocurrency trading: a comprehensive survey. https://doi.org/10.1186/s40854-021-00321-6

33. Andrew J. G. Cairns, David Blake, Kevin Dowd (2006). Pricing Death: Frameworks for the Valuation and Securitization of Mortality Risk. https://doi.org/10.1017/s0515036100014410

34. Markus K. Brunnermeier (2008). Deciphering the Liquidity and Credit Crunch 2007-08. https://doi.org/10.3386/w14612

35. Rebecca Bowman, Sophia Battaglia, Kara Morris et al. (2003). The Stochastic Programming Approach to Asset, Liability, and Wealth Management. https://doi.org/10.2470/rf.v2003.n3.3924

36. Lenos Trigeorgis, Andrianos E. Tsekrekos (2017). Real Options in Operations Research: A Review. https://doi.org/10.1016/j.ejor.2017.11.055

37. Malcolm Baker, Jeffrey Wurgler (2011). Behavioral Corporate Finance: An Updated Survey. https://doi.org/10.3386/w17333

38. Steven L. Schwarcz (2009). Regulating Complexity in Financial Markets. https://openalex.org/W1696081749

39. Amir E. Khandani, Andrew W. Lo, Robert Merton (2009). Systemic Risk and the Refinancing Ratchet Effect. https://doi.org/10.3386/w15362

40. Kristina Šutienė, Peter Schwendner, Ciprian Șipoș et al. (2024). Enhancing portfolio management using artificial intelligence: literature review. https://doi.org/10.3389/frai.2024.1371502

41. David S. Bates (1995). 20 Testing option pricing models. https://doi.org/10.1016/s0169-7161(96)14022-0

42. Marco Rocco (2012). Extreme Value Theory for Finance: A Survey. https://doi.org/10.2139/ssrn.1998740

43. Michael W. Brandt, Pedro Santa-Clara, Rossen Valkanov (2004). Parametric Portfolio Policies: Exploiting Characteristics in the Cross Section of Equity Returns. https://doi.org/10.3386/w10996

44. Richard A. Lewin, Stephen Satchell (2001). The Derivation of a New Model of Equity Duration. https://doi.org/10.17863/cam.5202

45. Zhiguo He, Bryan Kelly, Asaf Manela (2017). Intermediary asset pricing: New evidence from many asset classes. https://doi.org/10.1016/j.jfineco.2017.08.002

46. Franklin R. Edwards (1999). Hedge Funds and the Collapse of Long-Term Capital Management. https://doi.org/10.1257/jep.13.2.189

47. Arvind Krishnamurthy (2010). How Debt Markets Have Malfunctioned in the Crisis. https://doi.org/10.1257/jep.24.1.3

48. Darrell Duffie (2010). The Failure Mechanics of Dealer Banks. https://doi.org/10.1257/jep.24.1.51

49. Adrian Gepp, Martina K. Linnenluecke, Terrence J. O'Neill et al. (2018). Big data techniques in auditing research and practice: Current trends and future opportunities. https://doi.org/10.1016/j.acclit.2017.05.003

50. Richard N. Cooper, Garry J. Schinasi (2006). Safeguarding Financial Stability: Theory and Practice. https://doi.org/10.2307/20031932

51. Masoud Rahiminezhad Galankashi, Farimah Mokhatab Rafiei, Maryam Ghezelbash (2020). Portfolio selection: a fuzzy-ANP approach. https://doi.org/10.1186/s40854-020-00175-4

52. Richard S. Grossman, Forrest Capie, Charles Goodhart et al. (1996). The Future of Central Banking: The Tercentenary Symposium of the Bank of England.. https://doi.org/10.2307/2235583

53. Mark Rubinstein (1987). Derivative Assets Analysis. https://doi.org/10.1257/jep.1.2.73

54. Söhnke M. Bartram, Jürgen Branke, Mehrshad Motahari (2020). Artificial Intelligence in Asset Management. https://doi.org/10.2139/ssrn.3692805

55. Carmen Reinhart, Andrew J. Felton (2008). The First Global Financial Crisis of the 21st Century. https://openalex.org/W1628064201

56. David Hirshleifer, Jianfeng Yu (2012). Asset Pricing in Production Economies with Extrapolative Expectations. https://doi.org/10.2139/ssrn.1785961

57. Brian M. Lucey, Samuel A. Vigne, Laura Ballester et al. (2017). Future directions in international financial integration research - A crowdsourced perspective. https://doi.org/10.1016/j.irfa.2017.10.008

58. Ian Martin (2016). What is the Expected Return on the Market? *. https://doi.org/10.1093/qje/qjw034

59. Nikitas Stamatopoulos, Daniel J. Egger, Yue Sun et al. (2020). Option Pricing using Quantum Computers. https://doi.org/10.22331/q-2020-07-06-291

60. Ben Hambly, Renyuan Xu, Huining Yang (2023). Recent advances in reinforcement learning in finance. https://doi.org/10.1111/mafi.12382

61. Salman Bahoo, Marco Cucculelli, Xhoana Goga et al. (2024). Artificial intelligence in Finance: a comprehensive review through bibliometric and content analysis. https://doi.org/10.1007/s43546-023-00618-x

62. Servaas Storm (2018). Financialization and Economic Development: A Debate on the Social Efficiency of Modern Finance. https://doi.org/10.1111/dech.12385

63. Arthur M. Okun, William Fellner, Michael L. Wachter (1975). Inflation: Its Mechanics and Welfare Costs. https://doi.org/10.2307/2534106

64. Qin Xiao (2006). Property market bubbles : some evidence from Seoul and Hong Kong. https://doi.org/10.32657/10356/2178

65. U. Lauferts (2012). Decisioneering in Nuclear Energy Systems : A Real Option View. https://openalex.org/W2120516296

66. Bruno Fânzeres dos Santos (2014). HEDGING RENEWABLE ENERGY SALES IN THE BRAZILIAN CONTRACT MARKET VIA ROBUST OPTIMIZATION. https://doi.org/10.17771/pucrio.acad.33385

67. Rogerio Batista Adelino (2023). Essays on market volatility. https://openalex.org/W7120414586

68. Shahid, Emaan (2025). Return predictability in equity options : a supervised machine learning analysis of delta-hedged call option returns. https://openalex.org/W7115618686

69. Daniel Thomson (2016). Hedge fund return attribution and performance forecasting using the Kalman filter. https://openalex.org/W2767191212

70. G. Qiu (2011). Understanding the complex dynamics of financial markets through microsimulation. https://openalex.org/W1916331422

71. Jukka Sihvonen (2013). Essays on information and externalities in financial markets. https://openalex.org/W3049528568

72. Samuel H; Cox, Yijia; Lin, Ruilin; Zuluaga Tian et al. (2014). PAPERS FROM ACTUARIAL JOURNALS WORLDWIDE. https://doi.org/10.1017/s1748499514000207

73. Takeo Hoshi, Anil Kashyap (1999). The Japanese Banking Crisis: Where Did It Come From and How Will It End?. https://doi.org/10.3386/w7250

74. Jiao Wang, Lima Zhao, Arnd Huchzermeier (2020). Operations-Finance Interface in Risk Management: Research Evolution and Opportunities. https://doi.org/10.1111/poms.13269

75. Kai-Yin Woo, Chulin Mai, Michael McAleer et al. (2020). Review on Efficiency and Anomalies in Stock Markets. https://doi.org/10.3390/economies8010020

76. Henry T. C. Hu, Peter L. Bernstein (1993). Misunderstood Derivatives: The Causes of Informational Failure and the Promise of Regulatory Incrementalism. https://doi.org/10.2307/796975

77. Vinay Patel, Tālis J. Putniņš, David Michayluk et al. (2019). Price discovery in stock and options markets. https://doi.org/10.1016/j.finmar.2019.100524

78. Martin J. Conyon, Nuno Fernandez, Miguel A. Ferreira et al. (2011). The Executive Compensation Controversy: A Transatlantic Analysis ∗. https://openalex.org/W2123495184

79. Takeo Hoshi, Anil Kashyap (1999). The Japanese Banking Crisis: Where Did It Come from and How Will It End?. https://doi.org/10.1086/654383

80. Jie Cao, Amit Goyal, Xiao Xiao et al. (2022). Implied Volatility Changes and Corporate Bond Returns. https://doi.org/10.1287/mnsc.2022.4379

81. Farhan Hassan Khan, Adnan Gutub (2007). Message Concealment Techniques using Image based Steganography. https://openalex.org/W2587267430

82. Ramazan Gençay, Aslihan Altay-Salih (2003). Degree of Mispricing with the Black-Scholes Model and Nonparametric Cures. https://openalex.org/W2098353406

83. Torben G. Andersen, Tim Bollerslev, Francis X. Diebold (2010). Parametric and Nonparametric Volatility Measurement. https://doi.org/10.1016/b978-0-444-50897-3.50005-5

84. Marco M. Sorge (2004). Stress-testing financial systems: an overview of current methodologies. https://openalex.org/W3124408991

85. Torben M. Andersen, Tim Bollerslev, Peter Christoffersen et al. (2005). Volatility Forecasting. https://doi.org/10.3386/w11188

86. Alejandro Bernales, Massimo Guidolin (2014). Can we forecast the implied volatility surface dynamics of equity options? Predictability and economic value tests. https://doi.org/10.1016/j.jbankfin.2014.06.002

87. Torben M. Andersen, Tim Bollerslev, Francis X. Diebold (2002). Parametric and Nonparametric Volatility Measurement. https://doi.org/10.3386/t0279

88. Sylvain Benoît, Jean-Édouard Colliard, Christophe Hurlin et al. (2015). Where the Risks Lie: A Survey on Systemic Risk. https://doi.org/10.2139/ssrn.2577961

89. Nick Ellison (2006). The Transformation of Welfare States?. https://doi.org/10.4324/9780203099490

90. Maurice Obstfeld (1995). 6. International Capital Mobility in the 1990s. https://doi.org/10.1515/9780691231136-009

91. Thomas J. Linsmeier, Neil D. Pearson, Linsmeier, Thomas J. et al. (1996). Risk measurement: an introduction to value at risk. https://doi.org/10.22004/ag.econ.14796

92. Claudio Borio (2011). Implementing the Macroprudential Approach to Financial Regulation and Supervision. https://doi.org/10.4337/9781849808712.00017

93. Ben Hambly, Renyuan Xu, Huining Yang (2021). Recent Advances in Reinforcement Learning in Finance. https://doi.org/10.2139/ssrn.3971071

94. U.S. Commodity Futures Trading Commission (2020). Managing Climate Risk in the U.S. Financial System. https://doi.org/10.5281/zenodo.5247742

95. Wayne R. Guay, John E. Core, David F. Larcker (2001). Executive Equity Compensation and Incentives: A Survey. https://doi.org/10.2139/ssrn.276425

96. Jens Carsten Jackwerth (2004). Option-Implied Risk-Neutral Distributions and Risk Aversion. https://doi.org/10.2470/rf.v2004.n1.3925

97. Byeong-Je An, Andrew Ang, Turan G. Bali et al. (2013). The Joint Cross Section of Stocks and Options. https://doi.org/10.3386/w19590

98. Markus K. Brunnermeier, Martin Oehmke (2012). Bubbles, Financial Crises, and Systemic Risk. https://doi.org/10.3386/w18398

99. Kenneth A. Bamberger (2009). Technologies of Compliance: Risk and Regulation in a Digital Age. https://openalex.org/W1560339290

100. Sugato Bhattacharyya, Vikram K. Nanda (2012). Portfolio Pumping, Trading Activity and Fund Performance. https://doi.org/10.1093/rof/rfs017

101. Jens Carsten Jackwerth (1996). Recovering Risk Aversion from Option Prices and Realized Returns. https://doi.org/10.2139/ssrn.7745

102. Shihao Gu, Bryan Kelly, Dacheng Xiu (2018). Empirical Asset Pricing via Machine Learning. https://doi.org/10.3386/w25398

103. Malcolm Baker, Richard S. Ruback, Jeffrey Wurgler (2004). Behavioral Corporate Finance: A Survey. https://doi.org/10.3386/w10863

104. Uğur Lel (2011). Currency hedging and corporate governance: A cross-country analysis. https://doi.org/10.1016/j.jcorpfin.2011.12.002

105. Michael Gapen, Dale F. Gray, Cheng Hoon Lim et al. (2008). Measuring and Analyzing Sovereign Risk with Contingent Claims. https://doi.org/10.1057/palgrave.imfsp.9450026

106. Yener Altunbaş, Leonardo Gambacorta, David Marqués-Ibáñez (2010). Does Monetary Policy Affect Bank Risk-Taking?. https://doi.org/10.2139/ssrn.1577075

107. Daniel J. Egger, Claudio Gambella, Jakub Marecek et al. (2020). Quantum Computing for Finance: State-of-the-Art and Future Prospects. https://doi.org/10.1109/tqe.2020.3030314

108. Zhiguo He, Arvind Krishnamurthy (2008). Intermediary Asset Pricing. https://doi.org/10.3386/w14517

109. Akib Mashrur, Wei Luo, Nayyar A. Zaidi et al. (2020). Machine Learning for Financial Risk Management: A Survey. https://doi.org/10.1109/access.2020.3036322

110. Victor Chang (2014). The Business Intelligence as a Service in the Cloud. https://doi.org/10.1016/j.future.2013.12.028

111. Molly Hellmuth, Daniel E. Osgood, Ulrich Hess et al. (2024). Index insurance and climate risk: prospects for development and disaster management. https://doi.org/10.7916/wp8p-v354

112. René García, Éric Ghysels, Éric Renault (2010). The Econometrics of Option Pricing. https://doi.org/10.1016/b978-0-444-50897-3.50012-2

113. Samuel A. Vigne, Brian M. Lucey, Fergal A. O’Connor et al. (2017). The financial economics of white precious metals — A survey. https://doi.org/10.1016/j.irfa.2017.04.006

114. Nicholas Stern, Philip Suttle, Eung Kim et al. (2000). global development finance. https://doi.org/10.2458/azu_acku_hg3881_g567_2003

115. International Monetary Fund (2005). Adopting the Euro in Central Europe: Challenges of the Next Step in European Integration. https://doi.org/10.5089/9781589063501.084

116. René García, Éric Ghysels, Éric Renault (2003). The Econometrics of Option Pricing. https://doi.org/10.2139/ssrn.463860

117. Jiling Cao, Guanghua Lian, Teh Raihana Nazirah Roslan (2016). Pricing variance swaps under stochastic volatility and stochastic interest rate. https://doi.org/10.1016/j.amc.2015.12.027

118. Fred Espen Benth, Martin Groth, Paul C. Kettler (2006). A QUASI-MONTE CARLO ALGORITHM FOR THE NORMAL INVERSE GAUSSIAN DISTRIBUTION AND VALUATION OF FINANCIAL DERIVATIVES. https://doi.org/10.1142/s0219024906003810

119. G ClarkeRoger, Imm, Futures General On et al. (1992). Options and Futures: A Tutorial. https://doi.org/10.2470/rf.v1992.n5.4438

120. Anne MacKay (2011). Pricing and Hedging Equity-Linked Products under Stochastic Volatility Models. https://openalex.org/W185650075

121. Georges Hübner (2016). Option replication and the performance of a market timer. https://doi.org/10.1108/sef-01-2015-0012

122. Reilly Pickard, Yuri Lawryshyn (2023). Deep Reinforcement Learning for Dynamic Stock Option Hedging: A Review. https://doi.org/10.3390/math11244943

123. Stanislav Dolgopolov (2010). Risks and Hedges of Providing Liquidity in Complex Securities: The Impact of Insider Trading on Options Market Makers. https://openalex.org/W1540328162

124. Raimonda Martinkutė-Kaulienė (2013). Sensitivity of Option Contracts. https://doi.org/10.3846/btp.2013.17

125. Nadia Theron (2007). Aspects of some exotic options. https://openalex.org/W2143474443

126. R. Abbate (2014). CSA Discounting: Impacts on Pricing and Risk of Commodity Derivatives. https://doi.org/10.4236/jfrm.2014.33011

127. Geert Lovink, Nathaniel Tkacz, Patricia de Vries (2015). Moneylab Reader: An Intervention in Digital Economy. https://openalex.org/W2775605881

128. Matteo Bagnara (2022). Asset Pricing and Machine Learning: A critical review. https://doi.org/10.1111/joes.12532

129. Jérôme Henry, Christoffer Kok, Adrien Amzallag et al. (2013). A Macro Stress Testing Framework for Assessing Systemic Risks in the Banking Sector. https://doi.org/10.2139/ssrn.2337894

130. LleoSébastien (2009). Risk Management: A Review. https://doi.org/10.2470/rflr.v4.n1.1

131. Guido Max Mantovani, Elisa Daniotti, Paolo Gurisatti (2011). In Search of Corporate Risk Measures to Complete Financial Reporting: The Case of the 'Caldarerie' - Industry. https://doi.org/10.2139/ssrn.1920275

132. Jian Guo, Saizhuo Wang, Lionel M. Ni et al. (2022). Quant 4.0: Engineering Quantitative Investment with Automated, Explainable and Knowledge-driven Artificial Intelligence. https://doi.org/10.48550/arxiv.2301.04020

133. Joerg Orgeldinger (2017). Critical Analysis of the New Basel Minimum Capital Requirements for Market Risk. https://doi.org/10.28991/esj-2017-01111

134. Gilneu F. A. Vivan, Benjamin Miranda Tabak (2007). A new proposal for collection and generation of information on financial institutions' risk: The case of derivatives. https://doi.org/10.1057/palgrave.jdhf.1850061

135. Smaranda Paun (1999). Sensitivities of value at risk for non-linear portfolios. https://openalex.org/W2748244316

136. Chimezie Peter Nnanwa (2019). Mathematical Analysis in Investment Theory: Applications to the Nigerian Stock Market. https://doi.org/10.7190/shu-thesis-00220

137. Monica Billio, Mila Getmansky, Andrew W. Lo et al. (2010). Econometric Measures of Systemic Risk in the Finance and Insurance Sectors. https://doi.org/10.3386/w16223

138. Nicholas Chan, Mila Getmansky, Shane M. Haas et al. (2005). Systemic Risk and Hedge Funds. https://doi.org/10.3386/w11200

139. Unknown author (2011). The Theory and Practice of Investment Management. https://doi.org/10.1002/9781118267028

140. Sheri M. Markose, Simone Giansante, Ali Rais Shaghaghi (2012). 'Too interconnected to fail' financial network of US CDS market: Topological fragility and systemic risk. https://doi.org/10.1016/j.jebo.2012.05.016

141. Martin Oehmke, Ádám Zawadowski (2015). Synthetic or Real? The Equilibrium Effects of Credit Default Swaps on Bond Markets. https://doi.org/10.1093/rfs/hhv047

142. Vikas Agarwal, Naveen D. Daniel, Narayan Y. Naik (2011). Do Hedge Funds Manage Their Reported Returns?. https://doi.org/10.1093/rfs/hhr058

143. Pauline Shum, Walid Hejazi, Edgar Haryanto et al. (2015). Intraday Share Price Volatility and Leveraged ETF Rebalancing. https://doi.org/10.1093/rof/rfv061

144. Gjergji Cici, Alexander Kempf, Alexander Puetz (2016). The Valuation of Hedge Funds' Equity Positions. https://doi.org/10.1017/s0022109016000351

145. Marcin Kacperczyk, Stijn Van Nieuwerburgh, Laura Veldkamp (2009). Rational Attention Allocation Over the Business Cycle. https://doi.org/10.3386/w15450

146. Internationaler Währungsfonds, Tomás Baliño, Adam Bennett et al. (n.d.). Monetary policy in dollarized economies. https://doi.org/10.5089/9781557757579.084

147. Zhaogang Song, Dacheng Xiu (2015). A tale of two option markets: Pricing kernels and volatility risk. https://doi.org/10.1016/j.jeconom.2015.06.024

148. Guanglian Hu, Yuguo Liu (2022). The Pricing of Volatility and Jump Risks in the Cross-Section of Index Option Returns. https://doi.org/10.1017/s0022109022000333

149. Lu Yan (2012). Risk Management Project. https://openalex.org/W3129831260

150. Mosab I. Tabash, Suzan Sameer Issa, Marwan Mansour et al. (2025). Ripples of Global Fear: Transmission of Investor Sentiment and Financial Stress to GCC Sectoral Stock Volatility. https://doi.org/10.3390/economies13110313

151. Andrea Vedolin (2012). Uncertainty and leveraged Lucas Trees: the cross section of equilibrium volatility risk premia. https://openalex.org/W3141088371

152. Selçuk Balı (2012). WEATHER DERIVATIVES and PRICING APPROACHES. https://openalex.org/W2999779753

153. David Yermack (2012). Tailspotting: Identifying and profiting from CEO vacation trips. https://doi.org/10.3386/w17940

154. Pei Peter Lung (2001). Information content in asymmetries of call and put currency options. https://openalex.org/W658682293

155. J. Scott Chaput (1999). An analysis of trading in options on Eurodollar futures : trade types, risks, and profits. https://openalex.org/W431898529

156. Richard Meese (1990). Currency Fluctuations in the Post-Bretton Woods Era. https://doi.org/10.1257/jep.4.1.117

157. Akira Ariyoshi, Andrei Kirilenko, Inci Ötker et al. (2000). Capital Controls: Country Experiences with Their Use and Liberalization. https://doi.org/10.5089/9781557758743.084

158. Paul Hilbers, Alfredo Leone, Mahinder Gill et al. (2000). Macroprudential Indicators of Financial System Soundness. https://doi.org/10.5089/9781557758910.084

159. International Monetary Fund (2002). Financial Soundness Indicators: Analytical Aspects and Country Practices. https://doi.org/10.5089/9781589060869.084

160. Tobias Adrian, Markus K. Brunnermeier (2011). CoVaR. https://doi.org/10.3386/w17454

161. Andrea Buraschi, Jens Carsten Jackwerth (2001). The Price of a Smile: Hedging and Spanning in Option Markets. https://doi.org/10.1093/rfs/14.2.495

162. Alessandro Beber, Michael W. Brandt (2008). Resolving Macroeconomic Uncertainty in Stock and Bond Markets. https://doi.org/10.1093/rof/rfn025

163. Monica Billio, Mila Getmansky, Andrew W. Lo et al. (2010). Measuring Systemic Risk in the Finance and Insurance Sectors. https://openalex.org/W2118733325

164. Charles Goodhart, Daniela Gabor, Jakob Vestergaard et al. (2014). Central Banking at a Crossroads : Europe and Beyond. https://doi.org/10.26530/oapen_626351

165. Andrea Buraschi, Jens Carsten Jackwerth (2001). The Price of a Smile: Hedging and Spanning in Option Markets. https://openalex.org/W3122700563

166. Feng Li (2006). Do Stock Market Investors Understand the Risk Sentiment of Corporate Annual Reports?. https://doi.org/10.2139/ssrn.898181

167. Robert F. Stambaugh, Jianfeng Yu, Yu Yuan (2012). Arbitrage Asymmetry and the Idiosyncratic Volatility Puzzle. https://doi.org/10.2139/ssrn.2155491

168. Kais Bouslah, Lawrence Kryzanowski, Bouchra M'Zali (2016). Social Performance and Firm Risk: Impact of the Financial Crisis. https://doi.org/10.1007/s10551-016-3017-x

169. Dirk Helbing, Stefano Balietti (2011). From social data mining to forecasting socio-economic crises. https://doi.org/10.1140/epjst/e2011-01401-8

170. Laurence B. Siegel, Barclay Douglas, Clifford Asness et al. (2003). Benchmarks and Investment Management. https://doi.org/10.2470/rf.v2003.n1.3922

171. Nicole Lee, Mary-Kate Brissett, Cindy Maisannes et al. (2010). Investment Management after the Global Financial Crisis. https://doi.org/10.2470/rf.v2010.n1.1

172. Jamie Morgan (2023). Systemic stablecoin and the brave new world of digital money. https://doi.org/10.1093/cje/beac060

173. Ben Caldecott, Elizabeth Harnett, Theodor Cojoianu et al. (2016). Stranded Assets: A Climate Risk Challenge. https://doi.org/10.18235/0012646

174. Stephen Smith, David Hess, Cindy Maisannes et al. (2009). Investing Separately in Alpha and Beta. https://doi.org/10.2470/rf.v2009.n3

175. Mila Getmansky, Peter Lee, Andrew W. Lo (2015). Hedge Funds: A Dynamic Industry In Transition. https://doi.org/10.3386/w21449

176. Anton Kajtazi, Andrea Moro (2018). The role of bitcoin in well diversified portfolios: A comparative global study. https://doi.org/10.1016/j.irfa.2018.10.003

177. Charlotte Wagner (2012). From Boom to Bust: How Different Has Microfinance Been from Traditional Banking?. https://doi.org/10.1111/j.1467-7679.2012.00571.x

178. Adalbert Winkler, Ursula Vogel (2010). Foreign Banks and Financial Stability in Emerging Markets: Evidence From the Global Financial Crisis. https://doi.org/10.2139/ssrn.1661727

179. Carsten Herrmann-Pillath, Alexander Libman, Xiaofan Yu (2010). State and market integration in China: A spatial econometrics approach to 'local protectionism'. https://openalex.org/W3124928357

180. Sarah Eaton, Genia Kostka (2013). Does Cadre Turnover Help or Hinder China's Green Rise? Evidence from Shanxi Province. https://doi.org/10.1057/9781137343680_3

181. Carsten Herrmann-Pillath (2010). Social capital, Chinese style: individualism, relational collectivism and the cultural embeddedness of the institutions–performance link. https://doi.org/10.1080/17538960903529568

182. Genia Kostka, Kyoung Shin (2011). Energy service companies in China: The role of social networks and trust. https://openalex.org/W1550720916

183. Carsten Herrmann-Pillath (2010). Meaning and function in the theory of consumer choice: dual selves in evolving networks. https://openalex.org/W3124259602

184. Peter Roßbach, Denis Karlow (2011). The stability of traditional measures of index tracking quality. https://openalex.org/W1582531904

185. Michael R. King, Carol L. Osler, Dagfinn Rime (2012). Foreign Exchange Market Structure, Players, and Evolution. https://doi.org/10.1002/9781118445785.ch1

186. Ravi Kashyap (2014). The Circle of Investment: Connecting the Dots of the Portfolio Management Cycle—Under the Purview of the

Uncertainty Principle of the Social Sciences. https://doi.org/10.5539/ijef.v6n5p244

187. Bradley Jones (2018). Central Bank Reserve Management and International Financial Stability-Some Post-Crisis Reflections. https://doi.org/10.5089/9781484342008.001

188. International Monetary Fund. Asia and Pacific Dept (2012). Australia. https://doi.org/10.5089/9781475572346.002

189. Ashley Bell, Julia Mackesson, Anh Viet Pham et al. (2016). Factor Investing and Asset Allocation: A Business Cycle Perspective. https://doi.org/10.2470/rf.v2016.n4.1

190. Momtchil Pojarliev, Richard M. Levich (2011). Is There Skill or Alpha in Currency Investing?. https://doi.org/10.2139/ssrn.1929106

191. International Monetary Fund. Monetary and Capital Markets Department (2022). United Kingdom: Financial Sector Assessment Program-Systemic Stress, and Climate-Related Financial Risks: Implications for Balance Sheet Resilience. https://doi.org/10.5089/9798400206504.002

192. OECD (2013). Annual Survey of Large Pension Funds and Public Pension Reserve Funds 2013. https://doi.org/10.1787/c2e0019a-en

193. John Y. Campbell (1995). Some Lessons from the Yield Curve. https://doi.org/10.1257/jep.9.3.129

194. Andrei Kirilenko, Andrew W. Lo (2013). Moore's Law versus Murphy's Law: Algorithmic Trading and Its Discontents. https://doi.org/10.1257/jep.27.2.51

195. Vikas Agarwal, Wei Jiang, Yuehua Tang et al. (2012). Uncovering Hedge Fund Skill from the Portfolio Holdings They Hide. https://doi.org/10.2139/ssrn.1787171

196. Michael Mussa, Giovanni Dell'Ariccia, Barry Eichengreen et al. (1998). Capital Account Liberalization: Theoretical and Practical Aspects. https://doi.org/10.5089/9781557757777.084

197. Tim Loughran, Bill McDonald (2020). Textual Analysis in Finance. https://doi.org/10.1146/annurev-financial-012820-032249

198. Rama Cont (2006). MODEL UNCERTAINTY AND ITS IMPACT ON THE PRICING OF DERIVATIVE INSTRUMENTS. https://doi.org/10.1111/j.1467-9965.2006.00281.x

199. Andrea Enria, Lorenzo Cappiello, Frank Dierick et al. (2004). Fair Value Accounting and Financial Stability. https://doi.org/10.2139/ssrn.749044

200. Alexandre Kossoy, Philippe Ambrosi (2010). State and Trends of the Carbon Market 2010. https://doi.org/10.1596/13401

201. Abby Pratt, Julia Mackesson, Anh Pham et al. (2016). Financial Market History: Reflections on the Past for Investors Today. https://doi.org/10.2470/rf.v2016.n3.1

202. Söhnke M. Bartram, Harald Lohre, Peter F. Pope et al. (2021). Navigating the factor zoo around the world: an institutional investor perspective. https://doi.org/10.1007/s11573-021-01035-y

203. Adil Rengim Cetingoz, Charles-Albert Lehalle (2025). Synthetic Data for Portfolios: A Throw of the Dice Will Never Abolish Chance. https://doi.org/10.48550/arxiv.2501.03993

204. Enrico Schumann (2010). Essays on practical financial optimisation. https://doi.org/10.13097/archive-ouverte/unige:14994

205. Rui Pedro Barbosa (2011). Agents in the market place an exploratory study on using intelligent agents to trade financial instruments. https://openalex.org/W129294831

206. Unknown author (2024). Check Your Understanding Answers. https://doi.org/10.1002/9781394308286.app

207. К. А. Н. Аданэн, K. A. N. Adanin (2025). Forecasting stock prices for agricultural commodities using machine learning. https://openalex.org/W7117213110

208. К. А. Н. Аданэн, K. A. N. Adanin (2025). Прогнозирование биржевых цен на сельхозтовары с использованием машинного обучения : магистерская диссертация. https://openalex.org/W7117283124

209. Vincent Gramlich, Tobias Guggenberger, Marc Principato et al. (2023). A multivocal literature review of decentralized finance: Current knowledge and future research avenues. https://doi.org/10.1007/s12525-023-00637-4

210. Burkhard Drees, Garry J. Schinasi, Charles Kramer et al. (2001). Modern Banking and OTC Derivatives Markets: The Transformation of Global Finance and its Implications for Systemic Risk. https://doi.org/10.5089/9781557759993.084

211. Erya Jiang, Bo Qin, Qing K. Wang et al. (2023). Decentralized Finance (DeFi): A Survey. https://doi.org/10.48550/arxiv.2308.05282

212. Unknown author (2025). Integrating Real-Time Financial Data Streams to Enhance Dynamic Risk Modeling and Portfolio Decision Accuracy. https://doi.org/10.7753/ijcatr1408.1001

213. Gregory Scopino (2014). Do Automated Trading Systems Dream of Manipulating the Price of Futures Contracts? Policing Markets for Improper Trading Practices by Algorithmic Robots. https://openalex.org/W1534682125

214. Ravi Kashyap (2023). A Tale of Two Currencies: Cash and Crypto. https://doi.org/10.48550/arxiv.2302.06348

215. Joyce Efekpogua Fiemotongha, Abbey Ngochindo Igwe, Chikezie Paul- Mikki Ewim et al. (2024). Mitigating market volatility: Advanced techniques for enhancing stability and profitability in energy commodities trading. https://doi.org/10.54660/ijmor.2024.3.131-148

216. International Monetary Fund (2016). Sri Lanka: Staff Report for the 2016 Article IV Consultation and Request for a Three-Year Extended Arrangement under the Extended Fund Facility-Press Release;

Staff Report; Staff Statement, and Statement by the Executive Director for Sri Lanka. https://doi.org/10.5089/9781475532388.002

217. Annalisa Ferrari (2025). Artificial intelligence and machine learning in finance: Addressing complex problems and ESG applications. https://doi.org/10.22495/aimlfacpea

218. Mark W. Allen, Christoph B. Rosenberg, Christian Keller et al. (2002). A Balance Sheet Approach to Financial Crisis. https://doi.org/10.2139/ssrn.880876

219. Mark W. Allen, Christoph B. Rosenberg, Christian Keller et al. (2002). A Balance Sheet Approach to Financial Crisis. https://doi.org/10.5089/9781451957150.001.a001

220. Tobias Adrian, Hyun Song Shin (2009). The shadow banking system: implications for fi nancial regulation. https://openalex.org/W3023030938

221. International Monetary Fund (2002). Capital Account Liberalization and Financial Sector Stability. https://doi.org/10.5089/9781589060852.084

222. Joon-Ho Hahm, Frederic S. Mishkin, Hyun Song Shin et al. (2012). Macroprudential Policies in Open Emerging Economies. https://doi.org/10.3386/w17780

223. Iman Anabtawi, Steven L. Schwarcz (2013). Regulating Ex Post: How Law Can Address the Inevitability of Financial Failure. https://openalex.org/W2122033093

224. Orit Halpern, Robert J. Mitchell (2023). The Smartness Mandate. https://doi.org/10.7551/mitpress/14623.001.0001

225. Renate Mayntz (2012). Crisis and control : institutional change in financial market regulation. https://openalex.org/W600924478

226. E. Philip Davis (2000). Portfolio regulation of life insurance companies and pension funds. https://openalex.org/W91447623

227. Luigi Zingales (2015). Does Finance Benefit Society?. https://doi.org/10.3386/w20894

228. Raffaele Della Croce (2011). Pension Funds Investment in Infrastructure. https://doi.org/10.1787/5kg272f9bnmx-en

229. International Monetary Fund (2022). Review of The Institutional View on The Liberalization and Management of Capital Flows. https://doi.org/10.5089/9798400204593.007

230. Viral V. Acharya, Richard Berner, Robert F. Engle et al. (2023). Climate Stress Testing. https://doi.org/10.1146/annurev-financial-110921-101555

231. Zhiguo He, Stefan Nagel, Zhaogang Song (2020). Treasury Inconvenience Yields during the COVID-19 Crisis. https://doi.org/10.3386/w27416

232. Ľuboš Pástor, Pietro Veronesi (2009). Learning in Financial Markets. https://doi.org/10.1146/annurev.financial.050808.114428

233. Pierre Collin-Dufresne, Vyacheslav Fos (2015). Do Prices Reveal the Presence of Informed Trading?. https://doi.org/10.1111/jofi.12260

234. Dimitri Vayanos (2004). Flight to Quality, Flight to Liquidity, and the Pricing of Risk. https://doi.org/10.3386/w10327

235. Bahattin Büyükşahin, Michael S. Haigh, Jeffrey H. Harris et al. (2008). Fundamentals, Trader Activity and Derivative Pricing. https://doi.org/10.2139/ssrn.966692

236. Paul L. Joskow (2003). The Difficult Transition to Competitive Electricity Markets in the U.S.. https://doi.org/10.17863/cam.5414

237. Joachim von Braun, Getaw Tadesse, Von Braun, Joachim et al. (2012). Global Food Price Volatility and Spikes: An Overview of Costs, Causes, and Solutions. https://doi.org/10.22004/ag.econ.120021

238. Matthias Kalkuhl, Joachim von Braun, Máximo Torero (2016). Volatile and Extreme Food Prices, Food Security, and Policy: An Overview. https://doi.org/10.1007/978-3-319-28201-5_1

239. Tania Salerno (2016). Cargill's corporate growth in times of crises: how agro-commodity traders are increasing profits in the midst of volatility. https://doi.org/10.1007/s10460-016-9681-8

240. Tino Kluge (2006). Pricing swing options and other electricity derivatives. https://doi.org/10.5287/ora-j5ogkorpr

241. Quang Nguyen, Trang Kim, Marina Papanastassiou (2017). Policy uncertainty, derivatives use, and firm-level FDI. https://doi.org/10.1057/s41267-017-0090-z

242. Saleem Bahaj, Ricardo Reis (2021). Central Bank Swap Lines: Evidence on the Effects of the Lender of Last Resort. https://doi.org/10.1093/restud/rdab074

243. Zongyuan Zoe Liu, Mihaela Papa (2022). Can BRICS De-dollarize the Global Financial System?. https://doi.org/10.1017/9781009029544

244. Grace Xing Hu, Jiang Wang (2022). A Review of China's Financial Markets. https://doi.org/10.1146/annurev-financial-111620-010537

245. Hafiz Hoque, Dimitris Andriosopoulos, Kostas Andriosopoulos et al. (2014). Bank regulation, risk and return: Evidence from the credit and sovereign debt crises. https://doi.org/10.1016/j.jbankfin.2014.06.003

246. Chen Liu, Serena Wu (2023). Green finance, sustainability disclosure and economic implications. https://doi.org/10.1108/frep-03-2022-0021

247. Yurii Fedyk, Christian Heyerdahl-Larsen, Johan Waldén (2012). Market Selection and Welfare in a Multi-asset Economy. https://doi.org/10.1093/rof/rfs009

248. Tobias Adrian, Adam B. Ashcraft (2013). shadow banking: a review of the literature. https://doi.org/10.1057/9780230226203.3890

249. Kee-Hong Bae (2012). Determinants of Local Currency Bonds and Foreign Holdings: Implications for Bond Market Development in the People's Republic of China. https://openalex.org/W2103468080

250. Saule T. Omarova (2018). New Tech v. New Deal: Fintech As A Systemic Phenomenon. https://doi.org/10.2139/ssrn.3224393

251. Harold S Bradley, Robert E. Litan (2010). Choking the Recovery: Why New Growth Companies Aren't Going Public and Unrecognized Risks of Future Market Disruptions. https://doi.org/10.2139/ssrn.1706174

252. John C. Coffee (2012). The political economy of Dodd-Frank: Why financial reform tends to be frustrated and systemic risk perpetuated. https://doi.org/10.1017/cbo9781139175821.005

253. Tobias Adrian, Adam B. Ashcraft (2012). Shadow Banking: A Review of the Literature. https://doi.org/10.1057/978-1-349-95121-5_2946-1

254. International Monetary Fund (2009). Fiscal Implications of the Global Economic and Financial Crisis. https://doi.org/10.5089/9781589068506.084

255. William Forbes, Robert Hudson, Len Skerratt et al. (2015). Which heuristics can aid financial-decision-making?. https://doi.org/10.1016/j.irfa.2015.07.002

256. International Monetary Fund (2012). Brazil: Financial System Stability Assessment. https://doi.org/10.5089/9781475506723.002

257. Merritt B. Fox, Gabriel V. Rauterberg, Lawrence R. Glosten (2015). The New Stock Market: Sense and Nonsense. https://doi.org/10.7916/d8df6qp5

258. Charles K. Whitehead (2010). Reframing Financial Regulation. https://openalex.org/W2164316180

259. Sandra Blome, Kai Fachinger, Dorothee Franzen et al. (2007). Pension Fund Regulation and Risk Management. https://doi.org/10.1787/171755452623

260. David Blake (2001). The United Kingdom pension system: key issues. https://openalex.org/W2152783737

261. International Monetary Fund (2011). Russian Federation: Financial System Stability Assessment. https://doi.org/10.5089/9781463904203.002

262. Jerry W. Markham (2021). Regulating Broker-Dealer Investment Recommendations—Laying the Groundwork for the Next Financial Crisis. https://openalex.org/W3166420226

263. Narcisa Roxana Moşteanu, Alessio Faccia (2021). Fintech Frontiers in Quantum Computing, Fractals, and Blockchain Distributed Ledger: Paradigm Shifts and Open Innovation. https://doi.org/10.3390/joitmc7010019

264. Huaqin Zhao, Zhengliang Liu, Zihao Wu et al. (2024). Revolutionizing Finance with LLMs: An Overview of Applications and Insights. https://doi.org/10.48550/arxiv.2401.11641

265. Bogdan Adamyk, Vladlena Benson, Oksana Adamyk et al. (2025). Risk Management in DeFi: Analyses of the Innovative Tools and Platforms for Tracking DeFi Transactions. https://doi.org/10.3390/jrfm18010038

266. Z. Al-Hamouz, Ali Sadiq Al-Faraj (2003). Transmission expansion planning using nonlinear programming. https://doi.org/10.1109/tdc.2002.1178259

267. Pablo Mac Clay, Roberto Feeney, Jorge Sellare (2024). Technology-driven transformations in agri-food global value chains: The role of incumbent firms from a corporate venture capital perspective. https://doi.org/10.1016/j.foodpol.2024.102684

268. Robyn Rae, Allison Barrett, David J. Brooks et al. (2018). A review of Solvency II: Has it met its objectives?. https://doi.org/10.1017/s1357321717000241

269. International Monetary Fund (2011). Possible Unintended Consequences of Basel III and Solvency II. https://doi.org/10.5089/9781462308279.001

270. Bühler, Hans (2006). Volatility Markets: Consistent Modeling, Hedging and Practical Implementation. https://doi.org/10.14279/depositonce-1411

271. Jiali Fang, Yafeng Qin, Ben Jacobsen (2014). Technical market indicators: An overview. https://doi.org/10.1016/j.jbef.2014.09.001

272. Turan G. Bali, Scott Murray (2013). Does Risk-Neutral Skewness Predict the Cross-Section of Equity Option Portfolio Returns?. https://doi.org/10.1017/s0022109013000410

273. Daniel Egloff, Markus Leippold, Liuren Wu (2010). The Term Structure of Variance Swap Rates and Optimal Variance Swap Investments. https://doi.org/10.1017/s0022109010000463

274. Kenniy Olorunnimbe, Herna L. Viktor (2022). Deep learning in the stock market—a systematic survey of practice, backtesting, and applications. https://doi.org/10.1007/s10462-022-10226-0

275. Mary Dowell-Jones, David Kinley (2011). Minding the Gap: Global Finance and Human Rights. https://doi.org/10.1017/s0892679411000062

276. John W. Bagby, Nizan Packin (2021). RegTech and Predictive Lawmaking: Closing the RegLag Between Prospective Regulated Activity and Regulation. https://doi.org/10.36639/mbelr.10.2.regtech

277. Alessi Lucia (2020). Joint JRC- EBA workshop on Banking Regulation and Sustainability. https://doi.org/10.2760/550084

278. Roy Black, Andreas Tsanakas, Andrew Smith et al. (2017). Model risk: illuminating the black box. https://doi.org/10.1017/s1357321717000150

279. Hajar Raouf (2018). Risk Governance, Financial Performance and Financial Stability: Comparative Studies between Conventional and Islamic Banks in the GCC Countries. https://openalex.org/W2883581681

280. International Monetary Fund (2005). Ukraine: 2005 Article IV Consultation and Ex Post Assessment of Longer-Term Program Engagement: Staff Reports; Staff Supplement; and Public Information Notice on the Executive Board Discussion. https://doi.org/10.5089/9781451839067.002

281. Mirzha de Manuel, Karel Lannoo (2013). Saving for Retirement and Investing for Growth. Report of the CEPS-RCMI Task Force on Long-term Investing and Retirement Savings. CEPS Task Force Report, September 2013. https://openalex.org/W650375245

282. Moreblessing Ngwenya (2017). Assessment of enterprise risk management maturity levels of the insurance industry in Botswana. https://openalex.org/W2799957343

283. Wendy L. Currie, Jonathan J. M. Seddon (2023). Competing stakeholder narratives on crypto-assets: Miracle or mirage?. https://doi.org/10.1177/02683962231202534

284. Christian Chamorro-Courtland (2012). The Trillion Dollar Question: Can a Central Bank Bail Out a Central Counterparty Clearing House Which is "Too Big to Fail"?. https://openalex.org/W3122875720

285. Stephen A. Deane, Olivier Fines (2023). Cryptoassets: Beyond the Hype. https://doi.org/10.56227/23.1.1

286. Damir Filipović (2005). Benchmarking Study of Internal Models. https://openalex.org/W560390716

287. Editha Creus, S Chandwani, P Mcconaghy et al. (2020). Assessing the Enabling Environment for Disaster Risk Financing: A Country Diagnostics Tool Kit. https://doi.org/10.22617/tcs200190-2

288. Joe Blankenship (2017). Forging Blockchains: Spatial Production and Political Economy of Decentralized Cryptocurrency Code/Spaces. https://openalex.org/W2621156711

289. Author-Name Alexander J. McNeil, Rüdiger Frey, Paul Embrechts (2015). Risk in Perspective. https://openalex.org/W2293419320

290. Jami Seitsonen (2018). The Possible Effect of Markets in Financial Instruments Directive 2 on High Frequency Trading. https://openalex.org/W2962416238

Conclusion

The most durable edge in derivatives is not the ability to forecast every move, but the ability to define exactly which uncertainty is being paid for, transferred, or hedged. That distinction matters because derivative markets reward precision more than conviction. A position that is loosely conceived may still produce a gain, but a position that is precisely specified can be evaluated, financed, monitored, and adjusted in a way that makes its risk contribution legible to the portfolio rather than hidden inside it.

That legibility is increasingly important in markets where the sources of return are harder to separate from the sources of fragility. Asset pricing research has shown that machine learning can improve the measurement of risk premiums across asset classes and, in some cases, materially enhance performance relative to traditional regression-based approaches [28]. The implication for derivatives is not that models replace judgment, but that the information set used to price, hedge, and rank exposures can be broadened without losing discipline. At the same time, the presence of a stronger model does not eliminate the need to ask whether the trade is executable, whether the hedge is stable, and whether the payoff still makes sense under stressed liquidity.

For experienced practitioners, the practical test is whether a derivative position improves the portfolio's structure rather than merely changing its appearance. A trade may reduce reported volatility while increasing gap risk. It may lower current margin usage while adding path dependence. It may convert a directional view into a spread that looks defined-risk on paper but still requires active management under adverse moves. The relevant question is not whether the instrument is sophisticated, but whether the exposure it creates is coherent with the objective the book is actually trying to achieve.

That coherence becomes especially important when derivatives are used across multiple functions at once. A hedge can also be a funding decision. A volatility position can also be a balance-sheet decision. A commodity overlay can also be a cash-flow decision. The same contract can serve different roles depending on whether the institution is a trader, a producer, a portfolio manager, or a risk officer. In practice, the best derivative programs are those that make these roles explicit instead of allowing them to blur together. The market does not punish complexity by itself; it punishes complexity that cannot be explained in terms of exposure, liquidity, and control.

Risk management therefore remains the central discipline even after the strategy is selected. The critical issue is not simply whether the position has a favorable expected value, but whether it can survive the combination of adverse price movement, widening spreads, financing pressure, and delayed re-hedging. A derivative book that is profitable in calm conditions but unstable in stress is not a robust source of edge. It is a latent source of forced behavior. The trader who understands this will evaluate positions not only by premium, delta, or implied volatility, but also by how quickly the book can be adjusted when the market becomes less cooperative.

That adjustment process is where quantitative tools and institutional judgment must remain in contact. Models can identify relative value, estimate sensitivities, and rank opportunities more consistently than intuition alone. But even strong models are conditional on the quality of the data, the stability of the regime, and the assumptions embedded in the execution process. A backtest may show attractive carry or convexity capture, yet the live result can differ materially once transaction costs, rebalancing frequency, and market impact are included. The book that survives is usually the one whose design anticipates those frictions before capital is committed.

There is also a broader market lesson: derivatives are not merely instruments for expressing views, but channels through which the financial system transmits stress, liquidity, and risk appetite. Measures of systemic vulnerability often depend on how institutions behave under distress rather than in isolation [160]. That means a position that appears benign at the desk level may still contribute to instability if many market participants are forced into similar hedges, margin calls, or de-risking responses at the same time. In that sense, the quality of a derivative strategy cannot be judged only by its standalone payoff. It must also be judged by its interaction with the rest of the market.

This is one reason derivatives remain central to modern finance even as the tools around them evolve. They allow institutions to separate risks that would otherwise be bundled together, to express views with capital efficiency, and to manage exposures that cash markets cannot isolate cleanly. They also expose the limits of any framework that treats price as the only relevant variable. In practice, the trader must be attentive to carry, convexity, funding, liquidity, and behavioral response all at once. The edge lies in seeing those dimensions together.

Behavior matters because markets are not driven by models alone. Investor expectations, institutional constraints, and feedback effects can all shape the path of prices and the demand for protection. Financial research has long shown that market behavior can depart from the simplest efficient-markets assumptions in persistent and meaningful ways [29]. For derivatives users, that means the premium embedded in an option or swap is not just a mathematical output; it is also a record of collective positioning, fear, hedging demand, and capital constraints. Reading that record well is often as important as pricing the contract itself.

At the same time, the institutional use of derivatives is increasingly tied to broader questions of balance-sheet management, regulation, and capital efficiency. Hedging decisions can affect debt capacity, tax position, and risk-bearing ability, which is why corporate users often treat derivatives as part of financial architecture rather than as isolated trades [21]. For asset managers and hedge funds, the same logic applies in a different form: the derivative is useful to the extent that it helps preserve the portfolio's intended exposures while making the book more resilient to adverse regimes.

The future of derivatives practice will likely reward firms that combine three capabilities: a clear economic objective, a rigorous quantitative process, and a governance structure that can keep pace with complexity. None of these is sufficient on its own. A sophisticated model without a mandate can produce elegant noise. A mandate without risk controls can produce hidden fragility. Controls without market understanding can produce paralysis. The strongest programs will be those that treat derivatives as a tool for disciplined exposure design, not as a substitute for it.

That is the standard by which the rest of the book should be read. Every structure, model, and hedge is ultimately judged by the same test: whether it improves the portfolio's ability to earn, preserve, or transfer risk under real market conditions. If it does, the derivative is serving its purpose. If it does not, the complexity is only cosmetic.

Appendix: Practical Reference Tools and Formula Guide

What follows is a compact working reference meant to support the trading, valuation, and risk discussions that precede it without repeating them. The purpose here is not to reopen the conceptual argument, but to place the most used relationships, payoff patterns, and review prompts into a form that can be consulted quickly when decisions have to be made under time pressure. In practice, the value of a reference section is measured by whether it reduces ambiguity at the point of execution: whether a spread is being sized correctly, whether a hedge has the intended sensitivity, whether a model input is being carried consistently, and whether the trade record is complete enough to survive later review. The material that follows is therefore organized for direct use, with formulas, comparisons, and checklists presented as tools rather than as a new layer of theory.

Key formulas and pricing relationships

For practical work, the first formulas to keep close are the ones that connect a derivative's quoted price to the no-arbitrage relationships underneath it. A forward or futures price is anchored by carry: spot adjusted for financing, income, and convenience or storage effects. In the simplest equity setting with a continuous dividend yield, the forward price can be expressed as $F = S e^{(r-q)T}$, where S is spot, r is the risk-free rate, q is the dividend yield, and T is time to maturity. For commodities, the same structure is often written with a convenience yield or storage cost in place of dividend income. The point is not that every market obeys one neat formula, but that the forward embeds the economic cost of carrying the underlying until delivery.

Put-call parity is the second relationship that belongs in any working reference because it ties together the prices of calls, puts, the underlying, and the strike. For European options on a non-dividend-paying asset, the parity relation is $C - P = S - K e^{-rT}$. With dividends or carry, the adjustment is straightforward in principle: the present value of expected distributions is subtracted from the spot leg. Parity is more than a textbook identity; it is a consistency check for markets, a way to infer one price from another, and a fast diagnostic for misalignment across strikes or expirations. Violations can arise from transaction costs, funding frictions, exercise style, or market dislocation, but the relationship remains the reference point against which executable prices are judged.

Option value itself is usually decomposed into intrinsic value and time value. For a call, intrinsic value at any moment is $\max(S - K, 0)$; for a put, it is $\max(K - S, 0)$. The premium above that amount is time value, which reflects the possibility that the option may become more valuable before expiration. This distinction matters because two options with identical intrinsic value can carry very different time values depending on volatility, carry, and time remaining. Time value is also what decays as expiration approaches, though not always smoothly and not always symmetrically across strikes. In practice, traders watch the interaction between time decay and moneyness rather than treating theta as a linear loss rate.

The Black-Scholes-Merton framework remains the standard benchmark for translating inputs into a theoretical option price. In its canonical form, the model prices a European call as $C = S e^{-qT} N(d_1) - K e^{-rT} N(d_2)$ and a put as $P = K e^{-rT} N(-d_2) - S e^{-qT} N(-d_1)$, where N is the standard normal cumulative distribution function. The terms d_1 and d_2 summarize the relationship between spot, strike, volatility, carry, and time. The value of the model is not that it predicts the market perfectly, but that it provides a coherent mapping from assumptions to price. That is why the equation became so central to modern finance: it turned a vague pricing problem into a disciplined one [24].

Implied volatility is the market's way of inverting that mapping. Instead of asking, "What price does the model produce if volatility is 20%?" the trader asks, "What volatility must be inserted so that the model matches the observed premium?" This inversion is useful because it expresses option prices in a common language across strikes and maturities. But implied volatility is not a forecast in the narrow sense; it is a state variable that bundles together expected realized volatility, risk premia, supply-demand imbalance, and hedging pressure. When the volatility surface slopes upward for downside puts or grows steeper in short-dated maturities, the message is not only about expected movement but also about the market's willingness to pay for protection.

Greeks are the next layer of relationships because they translate price into sensitivity. Delta is the first derivative of option value with respect to the underlying; gamma is the rate at which delta changes; theta is the rate of change with time; vega measures sensitivity to volatility; and rho measures sensitivity to rates. Written compactly, these partial derivatives are the bridge between a static quote and a dynamic risk profile. A portfolio that is delta-neutral at one moment may not remain so after a small move, because gamma continuously changes the hedge ratio. Likewise, a position that appears insensitive to volatility in one regime can become highly exposed if the surface shifts. These relationships are why professional books are monitored in terms of exposures, not just mark-to-market.

Several additional pricing relationships are worth keeping in view because they often explain the gap between theoretical and executable values. Early exercise is rarely optimal for non-dividend-paying American calls, but it can matter for puts and for options on dividend-paying assets when the present value of the dividend exceeds the remaining time value. The cost of carry, financing terms, and borrow availability can all alter the effective parity relationship. In stressed markets, the price of protection can also reflect liquidity conditions rather than pure volatility expectations; research on market stress and liquidity preference shows that funding and balance-sheet constraints can materially affect asset pricing [234], and option markets are no exception. Option prices therefore encode not only beliefs about the underlying, but also the cost of trading and hedging that belief.

For cross-asset work, the most useful habit is to treat these formulas as linked identities rather than isolated equations. Spot, forward, discounting, implied volatility, and Greeks all describe the same contract from different angles. When the relationships line up, pricing is internally consistent; when they do not, the discrepancy may be a trading signal, a hedging cost, or a warning that the market is strained. In that sense, the formulas are not merely computational tools. They are the language used to determine whether an observed premium is a fair exchange for the risk being assumed, transferred, or embedded in the structure.

Strategy payoff summaries and comparison tables

Payoff summaries are most useful when they reduce a structure to its terminal economics without stripping away the features that matter in trade selection. A professional comparison table should answer four questions at once: what the position gains from direction, what it gains or loses from volatility, what the maximum loss or gain is, and what the trader must do to maintain it. That is why payoff summaries are best read alongside the contract's Greeks, margin treatment, and liquidity profile. Two structures can have similar profit zones at expiration and still behave very differently in the interim because one carries positive gamma, another is short volatility, and a third requires active rolling to preserve its intended shape. The table is therefore not a substitute for analysis; it is the compact form of analysis after the key assumptions have already been made explicit.

For a long call, the payoff profile is straightforward: limited downside equal to premium paid, unlimited upside, positive delta, positive gamma, and negative theta. The position benefits when the underlying rises enough and fast enough to overcome decay. For a long put, the mirror image applies: limited downside equal to premium, substantial downside participation in the underlying, positive gamma, and negative theta. These are the simplest examples of convexity purchased outright. Their value in a comparison table is not merely that they are easy to understand, but that they establish the baseline against which spread structures, collars, and synthetic positions can be judged. Any strategy that sells part of this convexity is, in effect, exchanging some combination of upside, downside, or time decay for a lower entry cost or a more favorable probability distribution.

Once premium collection enters the design, the table must show where the hidden obligations sit. A covered call, for example, typically offers limited upside above the strike plus premium received, modest downside protection from the collected premium, and a profile that is short volatility and short convexity relative to outright stock ownership. A cash-secured put is economically similar to a limit order to buy the stock at an effective lower price, but the obligation remains contingent on a decline in the underlying. Vertical spreads make the trade-off more explicit: the long vertical caps both gain and loss, while the short vertical does the opposite. In each case, the comparison should note not just the maximum profit and maximum loss, but also the breakeven point, the width of the profitable region, and whether assignment or exercise can alter the realized path before expiration.

Volatility structures deserve special treatment because their payoff summaries can be misleading if viewed only at expiration. A long straddle or strangle has a defined maximum loss equal to premium paid and theoretically large upside if the underlying moves far enough in either direction, but that description hides the fact that the position is also a bet on realized movement arriving before time decay overwhelms the premium. The table should therefore distinguish between terminal payoff and path dependency. Calendar spreads, for instance, may look neutral at initiation because the trader is buying one maturity and selling another, yet the economics depend on the term structure of implied volatility, the speed of decay in the front month, and the stability of the underlying around the strike. A structure that appears balanced on paper can still be highly sensitive to vol shifts or event timing.

Defined-risk structures are often easiest to compare when the table is organized around payoff shape rather than contract labels. A butterfly concentrates exposure around a narrow price zone and is typically used when the trader wants to express a view on pinning or bounded movement near a target strike. A condor widens that range and reduces the concentration of the payoff peak. A collar exchanges upside for downside protection and is often used when the economic objective is to preserve ownership while narrowing the distribution of outcomes. In each case, the key question is not whether the position is bullish or bearish in a broad sense, but how much of the underlying's range the trader is willing to monetize, insure, or cap. The payoff summary should make that boundary visible immediately.

Comparison tables are also the right place to flag the operational features that determine whether a strategy is suitable for a specific book. American-style options can be exercised early, which matters for dividend capture, deep-in-the-money calls, and short-option assignment risk. European-style options remove that timing uncertainty but may be less flexible for holders who want to react before expiration. Cash settlement versus physical delivery changes whether the trader must source or deliver the underlying. Exchange-listed contracts may offer better transparency and lower counterparty risk, while OTC structures may provide customization at the cost of documentation, collateral, and valuation complexity. In institutional settings, these differences are not footnotes; they often determine whether the strategy can be executed, margined, and unwound at acceptable cost.

A useful comparison table usually compresses the strategy into a consistent set of columns: market view, premium paid or received, maximum gain, maximum loss, breakeven, sensitivity to time decay, sensitivity to volatility, assignment risk, and typical use case. That format allows the reader to compare unlike structures without confusing them. A long call and a short put may both express bullishness, but one is a defined-risk premium outlay and the other is an obligation to buy on weakness. A short straddle and a short strangle may both harvest premium, but one carries tighter strike exposure and greater probability of early stress near the money, while the other sacrifices premium income for more room before losses accelerate. The table should make those distinctions visible in a way that supports pre-trade selection, not post-trade rationalization.

For advanced users, the most valuable payoff summaries are the ones that link the terminal diagram to the portfolio question underneath it. A structure that looks attractive in isolation may be inappropriate if it adds short gamma to an already fragile book, consumes too much margin, or concentrates losses in the same scenario that hurts the rest of the portfolio. Conversely, a payoff that seems modest on an isolated chart may be highly efficient if it neutralizes a specific risk factor or improves the distribution of outcomes under stress. In that sense, the comparison table is not only a teaching device; it is a translation layer between strategy design and risk governance. It lets the trader see, at a glance, which contract is being used to buy convexity, sell it, defer it, or reshape it into a form the portfolio can actually carry.

Risk checklist and trade review template

A disciplined review begins before the order is sent. The first question is whether the trade matches a clearly defined objective: directional exposure, volatility expression, income generation, hedge replacement, or portfolio insurance. If the purpose cannot be stated in one sentence, the position is usually carrying more ambiguity than edge. The second question is whether the instrument is the right vehicle for that objective. A trader may have the correct market view and still choose a structure whose payoff, margin profile, or liquidity is mismatched to the intended holding period. This is where a checklist earns its value: it forces the trade to survive a sequence of basic tests before capital is committed.

A useful pre-trade risk checklist starts with exposure identification. What exactly is being bought, sold, or transferred? Directional risk should be separated from volatility risk, and both should be separated from event risk, financing risk, and liquidity risk. The position should also be mapped to the portfolio it will sit inside, not evaluated as if it were isolated. A trade that looks modest on a standalone basis can become material once aggregated with existing delta, gamma, vega, correlation, or basis exposures. For that reason, the checklist should require a clear answer to whether the new position increases concentration, offsets an existing vulnerability, or simply adds another layer of complexity without improving the risk budget.

The next block of questions should address structure and execution. Are the strike, expiration, style, and contract size aligned with the forecast horizon and the intended exit plan? Is the position liquid enough to enter, adjust, and exit without relying on a perfect market? What is the realistic bid-ask cost, and how sensitive is the trade to a wider spread or a slower fill? If the strategy depends on rolling, rehedging, or dynamic adjustment, the checklist should specify when those actions will be taken and what market conditions would trigger them. Many derivative losses are not caused by the original thesis being wrong; they arise because the thesis required an execution quality or rebalancing discipline that the desk could not actually sustain.

Risk budgeting should be explicit and numeric. Before the trade is approved, the desk should know the maximum premium at risk, the likely margin requirement, the expected carry, and the loss threshold that would require review or reduction. For positions with nonlinear exposure, the checklist should include scenario outcomes rather than a single point estimate. A short option position, for example, should be tested against gap moves, volatility expansion, and time decay under adverse price paths. A long option position should be tested for theta bleed, implied volatility compression, and the probability that the market moves, but not fast enough. These checks are not substitutes for judgment; they are a way to ensure that judgment is being applied to the right failure modes.

Model and data review belong on the same list, because many derivative trades are priced, screened, or hedged through quantitative assumptions that can drift away from live market behavior. If a model is used to estimate fair value, hedge ratios, expected volatility, or scenario loss, the trader should ask whether the inputs are current, whether the calibration is stable, and whether the output has been stress-tested against alternative assumptions. Model risk is not confined to exotic structures; even plain-vanilla positions can be misread if the underlying distribution, dividend assumption, funding rate, or volatility surface is stale or oversimplified [278]. A good checklist therefore asks not only what the model says, but how much the trade depends on the model being right.

Counterparty, legal, and operational checks are equally important. Is the trade cleared, bilaterally documented, or subject to collateral terms that could change its economics under stress? Are the booking instructions, product identifiers, and settlement conventions unambiguous? Does the position create any documentation asymmetry between front office intent and legal enforceability? In institutional environments, these details are not administrative afterthoughts; they determine whether the risk transfer is real, enforceable, and observable. Governance frameworks that connect risk appetite, controls, and accountability are consistently associated with more resilient financial operations [279] [282].

The trade review template should mirror the checklist but shift from approval to accountability. After execution, the desk should record the original thesis, the actual fill quality, the initial and current Greeks or risk measures, the realized P&L drivers, and any deviations from the plan. It should also note whether the trade behaved as expected under the first meaningful market move. Did the position respond through direction, volatility, carry, or some unintended channel? Were hedges adjusted on schedule? Did liquidity, financing, or margin change the risk profile after entry? This type of post-trade review is especially valuable because it distinguishes a good idea that was badly implemented from a weak idea that happened to work in a favorable tape.

A practical review template can be kept compact if it is structured around a few recurring fields:

• Trade objective: what outcome the position is meant to achieve.

• Instrument and structure: underlying, strike, expiration, style, and size.

• Primary risks: direction, volatility, time decay, liquidity, funding, and counterparty.

• Scenario review: best case, base case, adverse move, and stress case.

• Hedge plan: what will be adjusted, when, and under what trigger.

• Execution quality: expected versus actual price, spread, and slippage.

• Post-trade observations: what the market did, what the model missed, and what should change next time.

The point of the template is not bureaucratic completeness. It is to make every derivative position answer the same set of questions in the same order, so that judgment can be compared across trades and over time. That consistency matters because the most dangerous positions are often not the most complex ones; they are the ones that were entered with confidence but never fully reviewed.

Glossary of essential derivatives terminology

A derivatives glossary is more than a convenience for terminology; it is a control surface for interpretation. In this field, small differences in wording often correspond to large differences in legal obligation, pricing treatment, margin behavior, or risk transfer. A trader who confuses exercise with assignment, or notional with premium, may still understand the broad idea of the position while missing the mechanism that determines how the position actually behaves when markets move. Precision matters because derivatives are contractual instruments first and financial expressions second. Their meaning is created not only by the underlying asset, but by the settlement convention, the exercise style, the margin regime, and the counterparty structure that surrounds them.

The term underlying refers to the reference asset, index, rate, commodity, or spread on which the derivative is based. The strike price is the fixed level at which an option holder may buy or sell that underlying. Premium is the price paid for the option itself, and it is distinct from the amount of exposure controlled by the contract. Notional value is the face amount used to define the economic scale of the contract; it is not necessarily cash that changes hands at initiation, but it is the base against which gains, losses, and sensitivities are often measured. Expiration is the date on which the contract ceases to exist, while maturity is the broader term for the end of contractual life, especially in instruments where cash flows or obligations continue until that date. Intrinsic value is the amount an option would be worth if exercised immediately; time value is the remainder of the premium, reflecting the possibility that the option may become more valuable before expiration.

Several terms describe how rights and obligations are converted into actual market transactions. Exercise is the act of invoking an option right. Assignment is the process by which an option writer is selected to fulfill the obligation created by exercise. American-style options may be exercised any time before expiration, while European-style options may be exercised only at expiration. Settlement is the method by which the contract is closed out economically. In physical settlement, the underlying is delivered or received; in cash settlement, only the net economic difference is paid. Open interest refers to the number of outstanding contracts that have not yet been offset or closed, and it is often used as a measure of market participation rather than immediate trading activity. Volume measures contracts traded over a given period, usually a day, and it can be high even when open interest remains unchanged if positions are opened and closed quickly.

Risk language in derivatives is built around the distinction between exposure and sensitivity. Delta measures the approximate change in option value for a small change in the underlying. Gamma measures how delta itself changes as the underlying moves. Theta captures the effect of time decay. Vega measures sensitivity to implied volatility. Rho measures sensitivity to interest rates. These are not isolated statistics; they are different projections of the same position into the variables that drive value. For that reason, a book can be directionally neutral and still be highly exposed to volatility, time decay, or financing shifts. A position can also appear small in notional terms while carrying large delta or gamma because the derivative's payoff shape magnifies the effect of market movement.

The glossary also needs terms that describe the market environment in which the contract trades. Implied volatility is the volatility level embedded in an option's market price, derived by solving the pricing model backward from observed premium. Realized volatility is the volatility actually observed in the underlying over a historical or forward-looking window. Volatility skew describes differences in implied volatility across strikes, while term structure describes differences across expirations. Bid-ask spread is the gap between the highest price a buyer is willing to pay and the lowest price a seller is willing to accept; in derivatives, that spread can be a meaningful part of the true cost of execution. Liquidity refers to the ability to trade size without materially moving price, but in derivatives it also depends on the depth of hedging markets, the availability of counterparties, and the ease of financing the position after execution.

A few terms carry special importance because they connect the contract to the broader financial system. Margin is collateral required to support a position, especially for futures, swaps, and short option exposure. Variation margin reflects daily or intraday gains and losses that are settled as the market moves. Initial margin is the collateral posted to cover potential future exposure. Counterparty risk is the possibility that the other side of the contract fails to perform. Clearinghouse or central counterparty is the intermediary that stands between buyer and seller in a cleared market, reducing bilateral credit exposure but introducing its own governance and systemic considerations [284]. In OTC markets, terms such as master agreement, netting, and collateralization are essential because they determine how exposures are legally aggregated and how losses are absorbed if a counterparty defaults.

Some of the most useful glossary entries are the ones that prevent conceptual confusion. Hedging is the deliberate reduction of an unwanted risk, not the elimination of all risk. Speculation is the assumption of risk for expected return. Arbitrage is the attempt to exploit a pricing inconsistency with limited directional exposure, though in practice transaction costs and model risk often make pure arbitrage rare. Convexity describes a payoff that changes nonlinearly with the underlying, which is why options behave so differently from linear instruments. Carry is the return or cost associated with holding a position through time, including financing, dividends, storage, or convenience yield. Basis is the difference between the cash price and the derivative price, or more generally between two related prices that should move together but do not perfectly converge. Roll refers to closing a position in one expiration and reopening it in another, a routine but economically important act in many institutional strategies.

The glossary should be read as an operating vocabulary, not a dictionary in the abstract. In practice, the same word can carry a slightly different emphasis depending on whether the user is a trader, risk manager, lawyer, accountant, or regulator. That is why disciplined derivatives work begins with terminology that is exact enough to support valuation, hedge design, documentation, and post-trade review. In a market where leverage compresses large exposures into small premiums and where settlement conventions can alter the economics of a position overnight, the vocabulary itself becomes part of the risk-control framework [289].

www.ingramcontent.com/pod-product-compliance
Lightning Source LLC
LaVergne TN
LVHW100308210926
848480LV00003B/1061

* 9 7 8 1 9 2 3 8 1 7 7 8 4 *